DAILY
DEVOTIONS
FOR
Women

DAILY
DEVOTIONS
FOR
Women

365
INSPIRATIONAL READINGS

HUMBLECREEK
INSPIRATION FOR LIFE

© 2006 by Barbour Publishing, Inc.

ISBN 1-59789-450-8

Compiled by Joanie Garborg.

Text is taken from *Daily Wisdom for Women* by Carol L. Fitzpatrick, published by Barbour Publishing, Inc. Some quotes have been edited slightly to help them stand alone.

Cover image © PhotoDisc

Scripture quotations unless otherwise noted are taken from the New American Standard Bible, © 1960, 1962, 1963, 1968, 1971, 1972, 1973, 1975, 1977, 1995 by the Lockman Foundation. Used by permission.

Scripture quotations marked NIV are taken from the HOLY BIBLE, NEW INTERNATIONAL VERSION®. NIV®. Copyright © 1973, 1978, 1984 by International Bible Society. Used by permission of Zondervan. All rights reserved.

Published by Humble Creek, P.O. Box 719, Uhrichsville, Ohio 44683

Printed in the United States of America.

5 4 3 2 1

JANUARY 1

So God created man in his own image,
in the image of God he created him;
male and female he created them.
Genesis 1:27 NIV

A whole new year stretches out before you, like a crisp carpet of newly fallen snow. What kind of footprints will you leave? Maybe your strides will be gigantic leaps of faith. Or perhaps you will take tiny steps of slow, steady progress. Some imprints might even be creative expressions, woman-sized angels in the snow.

JANUARY 2

When the woman saw that the tree
was good for food, and that it was
a delight to the eyes,
and that the tree was desirable
to make one wise,
she took from its fruit and ate.
Genesis 3:6

Two thousand years later, Jesus returned to another garden as His place of prayer. And on the cross the sacrifice of His life provided forgiveness, once again allowing access to God's presence. . .now within a spiritual garden of prayer.

JANUARY 3

To receive instruction in wise behavior,
Righteousness, justice and equity;
To give prudence to the naive,
To the youth knowledge and discretion,
A wise man will hear and increase in learning,
And a man of understanding will acquire wise counsel,
To understand a proverb and a figure,
The words of the wise and their riddles.
Proverbs 1:3–6

Lord, surround me with friends who know You and Your Word. Surround me in a crisis so I can still hear Your voice of wisdom and reason.

JANUARY 4

I have set my rainbow in the clouds,
and it will be the sign of the covenant
between me and the earth.
Genesis 9:13 NIV

Every day God freely displays His blessings. Are we too busy or disinterested to appreciate their wonder? Even if we've forgotten He's there, reminders are all around for He is the God of covenants. In a world where promises (or covenants) are disregarded routinely, we need God's kind of stability.

JANUARY 5

"Come, follow me," Jesus said,
"and I will make you fishers of men."
Matthew 4:19 *NIV*

Jesus came not only to save but to teach men and women how to have true servants' hearts. The substance of ministry is service. When the apostles agreed to follow Christ, they accepted the call on His terms, not theirs.

JANUARY 6

In the morning, O LORD,
you hear my voice; in the morning
I lay my requests before you
and wait in expectation.
Psalm 5:3 *NIV*

Lord, I wander around like those who have no hope, forgetting to ask You for wise solutions to my dilemmas. Help me remember to come to You before I start my day.

JANUARY 7

"Then I will bless her,
and she shall be a mother of nations;
kings of peoples will come from her."
Genesis 17:16

Lord, only You have the power to override earthly impossibilities. I pray today that no matter what appears to be impossible in my life, I'll be able to surrender it to Your care and trust.

JANUARY 8

And when you are praying,
do not use meaningless repetition
as the Gentiles do, for they suppose
that they will be heard for their many words.
Matthew 6:7

Your prayers certainly don't have to be elaborate or polished. God does not judge your way with words. He knows your heart. He wants to hear from you. His Word says that your prayers rise up to heaven like incense from the earth. Remember to send a sweet savor His way daily.

JANUARY 9

For the LORD gives wisdom;
From His mouth come knowledge
and understanding.
He stores up sound wisdom
for the upright; He is a shield
to those who walk in integrity.
Proverbs 2:6–8

God's Word says wisdom is truly a gift since it comes from the mouth of God, from the very words He speaks. Know that if you hold fast to the precepts contained in the Bible, you will walk in integrity.

JANUARY 10

And the LORD said, "The outcry of Sodom
and Gomorrah is indeed great,
and their sin is exceedingly grave."
Genesis 18:20

Lord, if I know someone caught in the deadly snare of sin, please remind me to pray for her. Only through You and Your Word can she truly be set free.

JANUARY 11

"For the gate is small,
and the way is narrow that leads to life,
and there are few who find it."
Matthew 7:14

*K*nowing the right answers and then taking them to heart is critical in our spiritual life. You can't get to heaven unless you are truly born again. Lord, give me Your light that I may respond.

JANUARY 12

"Beware of the false prophets, who come to you
in sheep's clothing, but inwardly are ravenous
wolves. You will know them by their fruits."
Matthew 7:15–16

*T*hose who abide in Christ preach the message that is consistent with the one Christ Himself taught. Lord, there are so many voices. Please help us to hear Yours, so that we won't be led astray.

JANUARY 13

When He got into the boat,
His disciples followed Him.
And behold, there arose a great storm on the sea,
so that the boat was being covered with the waves;
but Jesus Himself was asleep.
Matthew 8:23–24

Jesus took the disciples to the height of the storm's raging fury, yet all the time He was with them. Yes, the storms of life will attempt to ravage me but Christ is there, amid the frenzy, ready to deliver by just the power of His Word.

JANUARY 14

The LORD is King forever and ever;
Nations have perished from His land.
Psalm 10:16

God's Son, Jesus Christ, lives forever within those who call upon His name. And despite the efforts of the evil one, Jesus will remain King and will one day soon come back to claim this earth for His own, forever and ever.

JANUARY 15

Upon the wicked He will rain snares;
Fire and brimstone and burning wind
will be the portion of their cup.
For the LORD is righteous;
He loves righteousness;
The upright will behold His face.
Psalm 11:6–7

To those who choose to obliterate from their minds any notion of a "real hell," God says it does exist. The flip side of hell, of course, is heaven, the place where the righteous will behold His face. Where will you choose to spend eternity?

JANUARY 16

Help, LORD, for the godly man ceases to be,
For the faithful disappear from
among the sons of men.
Psalm 12:1

Lord, I have watched people carry burdens that humanly speaking should be unbearable. Yet with these trials You give them incredible joy. I praise You for all You are!

JANUARY 17

The people who walk in darkness
Will see a great light;
Those who live in a dark land,
The light will shine on them.
Isaiah 9:2

Lord, make the desire of my heart to seek and know You better. Take my life and use me for Your purposes.

JANUARY 18

"Therefore every one who confesses
Me before men,
I will also confess him before
My Father who is in heaven."
Matthew 10:32

If we know Jesus Christ and have responded to His invitation to receive Him as Savior, Jesus remains forever our advocate before the Father, saying with love, "She's mine." Know that you are so precious to Jesus that He gave His life for you. Doesn't it feel incredible to have Jesus as your defender?

JANUARY 19

Now Joseph was well-built and handsome,
and after a while his master's wife
took notice of Joseph and said,
"Come to bed with me!"
But he refused.
Genesis 39:6–8 NIV

Lord, I can't look ahead to see how a critical moment of obedience fits into Your overall plan. Please give me Your strength when my human desires threaten to overpower me.

JANUARY 20

And the disciples came
and said to Him,
"Why do You speak to them in parables?"
Matthew 13:10

He spoke in parables, or words of truth hidden under an imaginary net. Only with the hand of faith could these followers lift a corner of the net and view the truth. Yet to those whom He knew would respond, He provided plain words. How open have you been to God's Word?

JANUARY 21

He came to His hometown
and began teaching them in their synagogue,
so that they were astonished, and said,
"Where did this man get this wisdom
and these miraculous powers?"
Matthew 13:54

Jesus came from God, full of wisdom. Those who stood with Him during His earthly ministry had true wisdom and understanding from God. They made up His true family of believers. Lord, even if my earthly family rejects me, You have promised to be there for me.

JANUARY 22

He reached down from on high
and took hold of me; he drew me out of deep waters.
He rescued me from my powerful enemy,
from my foes, who were too strong for me.
Psalm 18:16–17 NIV

The very nature and character of God demands that He rescue those whom He loves. He reaches out to us with His mighty hand of rescue. When confronted with a crisis, like David, you can put your life in His hands.

JANUARY 23

"I am God, the God of your father," he said.
"Do not be afraid to go down to Egypt,
for I will make you into a great nation there.
I will go down to Egypt with you,
and I will surely bring you back again."
Genesis 46:3–4 NIV

Lord, You are a God who fulfills promises. I praise You!

JANUARY 24

And he said, "I am your brother Joseph,
whom you sold into Egypt.
Now do not be grieved or angry
with yourselves, because you sold me here,
for God sent me before you to preserve life."
Genesis 45:4–5

Lord, show me the brilliance of Your forgiveness that I might trust You in the trial and not miss the outcome You've planned.

JANUARY 25

"How is it that you do not understand
that I did not speak to you concerning bread?
But beware of the leaven of the
Pharisees and Sadducees."
Matthew 16:11

Jesus used a physical reality to get across a spiritual truth. But the disciples missed the point. His warning concerned the teaching of their religious leaders, men who knew the scriptures and yet denied Jesus as the Messiah. Lord, please expand the little faith I have and provide me with real comprehension.

JANUARY 26

The man said, "Who made you
ruler and judge over us?
Are you thinking of killing me
as you killed the Egyptian?"
Then Moses was afraid and thought,
"What I did must have become known."
Exodus 2:14 NIV

Moses felt unworthy to serve God because of his great sin. But instead of rebuke, Moses hears, "I will be with you . . .I am who I am" (Exodus 3:12–14 NIV). This is the same "I Am" who calls you to serve Him today.

JANUARY 27

"But what about you?" he asked.
"Who do you say I am?" Simon Peter answered,
"You are the Christ, the Son of the living God."
Matthew 16:15–16 NIV

Jesus repeatedly asked this question to those who followed after Him. He knew that in a short while He would be gone, and all these fledgling Christians would have to bolster their faith were His words and actions. Jesus wanted to be sure they would not allow the world's viewpoint to diminish who He was.

JANUARY 28

My God, my God, why have
You forsaken me?
Far from my deliverance
are the words of my groaning.
Psalm 22:1

Where are you today? On the road, walking toward Him? Sitting down, too bewildered to even formulate questions? Or are you kneeling right at His bleeding feet?

JANUARY 29

Then Moses said to the LORD,
"Please, Lord, I have never been eloquent,
neither recently nor in time past,
nor since You hast spoken to Your servant;
for I am slow of speech and slow of tongue."
Exodus 4:10

*T*he Lord wanted Moses to understand that He could and would meet all of his needs. Instead, Moses settled for allowing Aaron to speak for him. Do you give the Lord part of your problem and then halfway through start solving it yourself?

JANUARY 30

Then Pharaoh sent for Moses and Aaron,
and said to them, "I have sinned this time;
the LORD is the righteous one,
and I and my people are the wicked ones."
Exodus 9:27

*L*ord, it's so easy to see Pharaoh's obstinate streak. Give me strength to admit when I'm wrong. Give me strength to come to You in repentance.

JANUARY 31

Then Peter said to Him,
"Behold, we have left everything
and followed You; what then will there be for us?"
Matthew 19:27

*L*ord, I can't even imagine what You have in store for me in heaven. Please keep me faithful to complete the duties You've called me to on earth.

FEBRUARY 1

A scoundrel and villain,
who goes about with a corrupt mouth,
who winks with his eye, signals with his feet
and motions with his fingers,
who plots evil with deceit in his heart—
he always stirs up dissension.
Proverbs 6:12–14 NIV

*L*ord, all around me are those who seek to divert the path of my life. Help me to stand firmly on Your unchanging Word. Help me to trust You, the Ancient of Days, who always remains the same.

FEBRUARY 2

*Slay the Passover lamb. You shall take
a bunch of hyssop and dip it in the blood
which is in the basin, and apply some
of the blood that is in the basin
to the lintel and the two doorposts;
and none of you shall go outside the door
of his house until morning.*
Exodus 12:21–22

Lord Jesus Christ, I thank You for being my promised Messiah and Passover Lamb. I thank You for Your sacrifice so that my sins could be forgiven.

FEBRUARY 3

*The LORD was going before them
in a pillar of cloud by day to lead them on the way,
and in a pillar of fire by night to give them light,
that they might travel by day and by night.
He did not take away the pillar of cloud by day,
nor the pillar of fire by night,
from before the people.*
Exodus 13:21–22

Lord, let me not forget that I have seen your power. Help me to continue walking in obedience to You.

FEBRUARY 4

*"The kingdom of heaven may be compared
to a king, who gave a wedding feast for his son.
And he sent out his slaves to call those
who had been invited to the wedding feast,
and they were unwilling to come."*
Matthew 22:2–3

When God sent His Son to earth, He invited all men and women to a wedding feast. Lord, You've invited me to dine with You. Let me graciously accept your righteousness as the "wedding clothes" you provide.

FEBRUARY 5

*"Remember the sabbath day, to keep it holy.
Six days you shall labor and do all your work,
but the seventh day is a sabbath of the LORD
your God; in it you shall not do any work."*
Exodus 20:8–10

In the very beginning of our marriage, my husband and I made a decision to honor God on Sunday. He has blessed us for this faithful commitment, providing weekly spiritual guidance and also giving our bodies and souls the rest they require.

FEBRUARY 6

You have turned for me my
mourning into dancing;
You have loosed my sackcloth
and girded me with gladness.
Psalm 30:11

At one time, there were many people whom I felt incapable of pardoning. God's name topped the list. But I finally surrendered my life to Christ, and God's power of forgiveness has turned my own mourning into dancing.

FEBRUARY 7

Does not wisdom call,
And understanding lift up her voice?
On top of the heights beside the way,
Where the paths meet, she takes her stand. . . .
For wisdom is better than jewels;
And all desirable things cannot compare with her.
Proverbs 8:1–2, 11

Notice in this passage that wisdom is a choice. We can walk right past it. Wisdom is at the very precipice of every decision. Lord, You lay before me a path of righteousness. Help me desire to walk with You!

FEBRUARY 8

"You shall make holy garments
for Aaron your brother, for glory and for beauty. . .
that he may minister as priest to Me."
Exodus 28:2, 4

*N*otice that the priests were appointed by God to minister directly to Him. God didn't want them to forget whom they served. Lord, Your Majesty is incredible. I know that the things of beauty on earth are but a glimpse of all that's in heaven.

FEBRUARY 9

Then Jesus said to them,
"You will all fall away because of Me this night," ...
But Peter said to Him,
"Even though all may fall away
because of You, I will never fall away."
Matthew 26:31–33

*L*ater that night, Peter would know without any doubt that Jesus had tried to warn him. Then he would look into those intense eyes and understand that because Christ went to Calvary, even this sin of denial could be forgiven.

FEBRUARY 10

When He set for the sea its boundary
So that the water would not transgress His command,
When He marked out the foundations of the earth;
Then I was beside Him, as a master workman.
Proverbs 8:29–30

Somehow we have turned around history. Humans are not in charge. God is. And He's still commanding the dawn to happen and the earth to keep spinning and the stars to remain in the sky. Aren't you glad?

FEBRUARY 11

Then the whole Israelite community
withdrew from Moses' presence,
and everyone who was willing
and whose heart moved him came
and brought an offering to the LORD
for the work on the Tent of Meeting,
for all its service.
Exodus 35:20–21 NIV

Lord, You've created within me something to be used to further Your kingdom. Please enable me to open my hands willingly in service.

FEBRUARY 12

*They spat on Him, and took the reed
and began to beat Him on the head.
After they had mocked Him,
they took the scarlet robe off Him
and put His own garments back on Him,
and led Him away to crucify Him.
Matthew 27:30–31*

Lord, You sacrificed all You had to provide my eternal salvation. Help me today to express true sorrow for my sins.

FEBRUARY 13

*Jesus came from Nazareth in Galilee
and was baptized by John in the Jordan.
Immediately coming up out of the water,
He saw the heavens opening,
and the Spirit like a dove descending upon Him;
and a voice came out of the heavens:
"You are My beloved Son,
in You I am well-pleased."
Mark 1:9–11*

Father, the picture can't be any clearer. Jesus is Your Son, and You are pleased with His perfect life and His perfect sacrifice for my sins.

FEBRUARY 14

Then the LORD called to Moses
and spoke to him from the tent of meeting, saying,
"Speak to the sons of Israel and say to them,
'When any man of you brings
an offering to the LORD,
you shall bring your offering of animals
from the herd or the flock.'"
Leviticus 1:1–2

Lord, how grateful I am for Jesus, Your unblemished Lamb. Might I willingly become a living sacrifice through service to You as I take the gospel to this needy world.

FEBRUARY 15

Now Simon's mother-in-law was lying
sick with a fever; and immediately
they spoke to Jesus about her.
And He came to her and raised her up,
taking her by the hand, and the fever left her,
and she waited on them.
Mark 1:30–31

Jesus meets every need for every situation if we come to Him in faith. Lord, thank You for always going well beyond what I expect or ask. I appreciate Your attention to priorities.

FEBRUARY 16

The woman of folly is boisterous,
She is naive and knows nothing.
She sits at the doorway of her house,
On a seat by the high places of the city,
Calling to those who pass by,
Who are making their paths straight:
"Whoever is naive let him turn in here,"
And to him who lacks understanding she says,
"Stolen water is sweet;
And bread eaten in secret is pleasant."
Proverbs 9:13–18

Lord, please guide me to the place you envision for me.

FEBRUARY 17

"Who are My mother and My brothers? ...
For whoever does the will of God,
he is My brother and sister and mother."
Mark 3:33, 35

As women, are we using our precious moments to further the gospel, or are we involved in trivial pursuits? Do we stand alongside those in our families who dare to make a difference? Or have we added to their burdens by missing their obvious purpose?

FEBRUARY 18

*A woman who had had a hemorrhage
for twelve years...after hearing about Jesus,
came up in the crowd behind Him,
and touched His cloak.
For she thought,
"If I just touch His garments,
I will get well."*
Mark 5:25, 27–28

Lord, You heal me when I come to You, by renewing my spirit and deepening my faith. I worship Your majesty and power.

FEBRUARY 19

*"Speak to the sons of Israel, saying,
'These are the creatures
which you may eat from all the animals
that are on the earth.'"*
Leviticus 11:2

Lord, Your call to obedience may not always make sense to me, but help me to remember that You have a reason.

FEBRUARY 20

For You formed my inward parts;
You wove me in my mother's womb.
I will give thanks to You, for I am fearfully
and wonderfully made; Wonderful are Your
works, And my soul knows it very well.
Psalm 139:13–14

God rejoiced at your birth. You were fashioned exactly the way He wanted you. How incredible to comprehend that when you awake in the morning, God is already thinking about you!

FEBRUARY 21

"LORD, make me to know my end,
And what is the extent of my days,
Let me know how transient I am."
Psalm 39:4

God wants us to trust Him for our future. To know our lifespan would affect us every day of our lives. So, God has guarded this secret as a great favor to us. To worry about the future is to be uncertain of your eternity.

FEBRUARY 22

The wise of heart will receive commands,
But a babbling fool will be ruined.
He who walks in integrity walks securely,
But he who perverts his ways will be found out.
Proverbs 10:8–9

Lord, help us to stress honesty, obedience, and the truth of Your Word, and to shower our kids with unconditional love so that our children can grow to maturity in a secure emotional place.

FEBRUARY 23

Jesus left that place and went
to the vicinity of Tyre. . . .
As soon as she heard about him,
a woman whose little daughter
was possessed by an evil spirit came and fell at his feet.
Mark 7:24–25 NIV

Jesus came to bring the Good News to the Jews first. But this woman, a Gentile with a demon-possessed daughter, says she needs Jesus' touch too. And He responds to her faith. Ask Jesus to touch your life this day.

FEBRUARY 24

*"You shall consecrate yourselves
therefore and be holy,
for I am the LORD your God.
You shall keep My statutes
and practice them;
I am the LORD who sanctifies you."
Leviticus 20:7–8*

Lord, having a relationship with You is the only way we can keep Your commands. Help us to relinquish our wills to You.

FEBRUARY 25

*Six days later,
Jesus took with Him Peter
and James and John. . . .
And He was transfigured before them;
and His garments became radiant
and exceedingly white, as no launderer
on earth can whiten them.
Mark 9:2–3*

When we come to believe in Him as Lord and Savior, Christ transforms us too, quickening our spirits, so that we are destined to spend eternity with God in heaven. It's a change on the inside which is displayed on the outside— for the unbelieving world to see.

FEBRUARY 26

*"From the beginning of creation,
God MADE THEM MALE AND FEMALE.
FOR THIS REASON A MAN SHALL LEAVE
HIS FATHER AND MOTHER, AND THE TWO SHALL
BECOME ONE FLESH; SO
they are no longer two, but one flesh.
What therefore God has joined together,
let no man separate."*
Mark 10:6–9

Lord, only You know the physical and mental abuse some married women have endured. Heal their pain and show them how to make wise choices. And forgive me when I miss Your best for me.

FEBRUARY 27

*"You shall have the fiftieth year
as a jubilee; you shall not sow,
nor reap its aftergrowth, nor
gather in from its untrimmed vines."*
Leviticus 25:11

Lord, Your ways are filled with wisdom. If only the world would realize Your majesty! On that day that You create a new heaven and earth, we will know what it really means to celebrate!

FEBRUARY 28

The memory of the righteous is blessed,
But the name of the wicked will rot.
Proverbs 10:7

To leave a rich legacy of love, one must be dearly acquainted with the Author of Love, our Heavenly Father. Lord, help me to live in such a worthy manner that I might be remembered as following after You all my days.

FEBRUARY 29

For we are His workmanship,
created in Christ Jesus for good works,
which God prepared beforehand,
so that we would walk in them.
Ephesians 2:10

Only when I came to Christ in a Christian commitment of faith, did I finally realize the importance of being a woman. All the talents and resources God has built into each one of us are essential—to love a husband, maintain a home, nurture children so they exhibit godly behavior, and perform specific tasks here on earth.

MARCH 1

*And again He took the twelve aside
and began to tell them what was going to happen to Him,
saying, "Behold, we are going up to Jerusalem,
and the Son of Man will be delivered to the chief priests
and the scribes; and they will condemn Him to death. . .
and three days later He will rise again."*
Mark 10:32–34

*L*ord, when grief overwhelms us let us remember Your death on Calvary's cross provides our hope of eternal life in heaven.

MARCH 2

*"Take a census of all the congregation of the sons of Israel,
by their families, by their fathers' households,
according to the number of names, every male,
head by head from twenty years old and upward,
whoever is able to go out to war in Israel,
you and Aaron shall number them by their armies."*
Numbers 1:2–3

*L*ord, with You everything has a plan. In a world that is filled with nebulous thinking, I can rely on Your consistency.

MARCH 3

The chief priests and the scribes and the elders came to Him,
and began saying to Him,
"By what authority are You doing these things,
or who gave You this authority
to do these things?"
Mark 11:27–28

Jesus Christ cannot be fooled. He knew the hearts of the Pharisees and scribes and He knows your heart too. Jesus, You spoke plainly about who You are. Help me hear.

MARCH 4

Again the LORD spoke to Moses, saying,
"Speak to the sons of Israel, and say to them,
'When a man or woman makes a special vow,
the vow of a Nazirite, to dedicate himself to the LORD,
he shall abstain from wine and strong drink.'"
Numbers 6:1–3

Whatever is preventing me from seeing only You, Lord, provide the strength I require to set it aside.

MARCH 5

And Jesus began to say,
as He taught in the temple,
"How is it that the scribes say
that the Christ is the son of David? . . .
David himself calls Him 'Lord';
and so in what sense is He his son?"
And the large crowd enjoyed listening to Him.
Mark 12:35–37

*A*m I like those in the crowd who simply "enjoyed listen-ing" to Christ? Help me take time to know You, Lord.

MARCH 6

The fear of the LORD prolongs life,
But the years of the wicked will be shortened.
The hope of the righteous is gladness,
But the expectation of the wicked perishes.
Proverbs 10:27–28

*I*nstead of being a cause of terror in our hearts, that phrase, "fear of the Lord" means to reverence and honor Him as God. God's very nature is goodness. Therefore, everything which stems from Him reflects His character. This knowl-edge should cause hope to flood our lives.

MARCH 7

Behold, I was brought forth in iniquity,
And in sin my mother conceived me.
Psalm 51:5

Admitting our own sinful state is the first step toward a more sincere Christian walk. And acknowledging the sin in our children makes us more effective Christian parents.

MARCH 8

Then the LORD came down
in a pillar of cloud and stood
at the doorway of the tent,
and He called Aaron and Miriam.
When they had both come forward,
He said, "Hear now My words:
If there is a prophet among you,
I, the LORD, shall make Myself known
to him in a vision.
I shall speak with him in a dream."
Numbers 12:5–6

Lord, although it's human to question things beyond my control, please help me understand that Your actions are always in my best interest.

MARCH 9

For there is one God,
and one mediator also
between God and men,
the man Christ Jesus,
who gave Himself as a ransom
for all.
1 Timothy 2:5–6

Lord, I believe in all that You are both God and Man.

MARCH 10

Now Korah. . .took action. . . .
They assembled together against Moses and Aaron,
and said to them, "You have gone far enough,
for all the congregation are holy, every one of them,
and the LORD is in their midst;
so why do you exalt yourselves
above the assembly of the LORD?"
Numbers 16:1–3

Like Korah, do you fight for control of your life? Surrender the ultimate control to God and realize the freedom of His perfect plan.

MARCH 11

Pilate answered them, saying,
"Do you want me to release for you the King of
the Jews?"... But the chief priests stirred up
the crowd to ask him to release
Barabbas for them instead....
They shouted back, "Crucify Him!"
Mark 15:9, 11, 13

What would I have shouted if I had been part of that crowd? And what affirmation do I give You today, Lord?

MARCH 12

Joseph of Arimathea came,
a prominent member of the Council,
who himself was waiting for the kingdom of God;
and he gathered up courage and went
in before Pilate, and asked for the body of Jesus.
Mark 15:43

Joseph was "a good and righteous man" (Luke 23:50–51). He had been born again through his faith in Christ. And knowing the scriptures concerning the death of his Savior, he prepared for it.

MARCH 13

*"Speak to the sons of Israel that they
bring you an unblemished red heifer
in which is no defect, and on which
a yoke has never been placed."
. . . And it shall be brought outside
the camp and be slaughtered.*
Numbers 19:2–3

*T*he purpose of everything God told the Israelites to do
was to point the way to Christ. Help me, Lord, to see the
Old Testament in light of the New Testament. For Christ
is the fulfillment of all I seek.

MARCH 14

*When I am afraid, I will put
my trust in You. In God,
whose word I praise,
In God I have put my trust;
I shall not be afraid.
What can mere man do to me?*
Psalm 56:3–4

*W*here do you go for refuge? I run to the arms of my
loving Father, just as David did in his own crisis. And He
always comes through. O Lord, You alone are my refuge
and strength.

MARCH 15

In the days of Herod, king of Judea,
there was a certain priest named Zacharias. . .
and he had a wife. . .and her name was Elizabeth.
They were both righteous in the sight of God,
walking blamelessly in all the commandments
and requirements of the Lord.
But they had no child, because Elizabeth
was barren, and they were both advanced in years.
Luke 1:5–7

What the world would have lost if Zacharias had become bitter over his circumstances! Lord, restore my hope in You today.

MARCH 16

So Israel joined themselves to Baal of Peor,
and the LORD was angry against Israel.
The LORD said to Moses,
"Take all the leaders of the people
and execute them in broad daylight before the LORD,
so that the fierce anger of the LORD
may turn away from Israel."
Numbers 25:3–4

Lord, shine Your beacon of truth on those who are in leadership, that they may never lead others astray.

MARCH 17

And there was a prophetess, Anna. . . .
She was advanced in years. . . .
She never left the temple,
serving night and day with fastings and prayers.
At that very moment she came up
and began giving thanks to God.
Luke 2:36–38

God had promised Anna that she would see the Messiah before she died. She waited eighty-four years, and He kept His Word. Let us strive to follow Anna's prayerful example, and we too will be blessed by God.

MARCH 18

Then the LORD spoke to Moses, saying,
"Among these the land shall be divided
for an inheritance according to the number of names."
Numbers 26:52–53

One day Christ Himself will return to claim the Holy Land for His people. He is coming back as the ultimate Judge and Rescuer of Israel. The time is now to be sure of our commitment to Jesus Christ and that of our loved ones.

MARCH 19

The word of God came to John,
the son of Zacharias, in the wilderness.
And he came into all the district around the Jordan,
preaching a baptism of repentance
for the forgiveness of sins.
Luke 3:2–3

John's exhortations were aimed at the "wilderness of men's souls." Many claim the faith yet exist in a wasteland of sin. Lord, help me to proclaim Your Word and love to anyone, anywhere.

MARCH 20

Hear my cry, O God; Give heed to my prayer.
From the end of the earth I call to You
when my heart is faint; Lead me to the rock
that is higher than I. For You have been a refuge for me,
A tower of strength against the enemy. . . .
Let me take refuge in the shelter of Your wings.
Psalm 61:1–4

Lord, I search for a way through the torrents of despair. How precious is the knowledge that You hear and care.

MARCH 21

*They journeyed from Rameses
in the first month, on the fifteenth day of the first month;
on the next day after the Passover the sons
of Israel started out boldly in the sight
of all the Egyptians, while the Egyptians
were burying all their firstborn.*
Numbers 33:3–4

At times, Israel's hardships made them long to be back in the bondage in Egypt. But much of their pain was because they refused to obey.

MARCH 22

*And Joseph awoke from his sleep
and did as the angel of the Lord
commanded him,
and took Mary as his wife.*
Matthew 1:24

Lord, we know that Joseph loved Mary and both were chosen by You. Yet they also obeyed You in their choice of a life partner.

MARCH 23

And the devil said to Him,
"If You are the Son of God,
tell this stone to become bread."
And Jesus answered him, "It is written,
'MAN SHALL NOT LIVE ON BREAD ALONE.'"
Luke 4:3–4

*H*ave you ever found yourself so tempted to sin that you ached all the way to your soul? Christ understands that pull toward evil. Lord, I thank You for Your Son's perfect victory over Satan.

MARCH 24

Shout joyfully to God, all the earth;
Sing the glory of His name;
Make His praise glorious.
Psalm 66:1–2

*D*avid knew that taking time to praise his awesome God provided strength and renewal for his weary soul. Lord, my grateful heart declares Your Name in a world that has all but forgotten that You still care and watch over the universe.

MARCH 25

*After that He went out and noticed a tax collector
named Levi sitting in the tax booth,
and He said to him, "Follow Me."
. . . And Levi gave a big reception for Him in his house;
and there was a great crowd of tax collectors
and other people who were reclining
at the table with them.*
Luke 5:27–29

*C*hrist's presence at this reception provided an opportunity for Him to share the gospel message. We too can seek out those whom society shuns and offer the compassion of Christ.

MARCH 26

*"The LORD your God has multiplied you,
and behold, you are this day as the stars of heaven in
number. May the LORD, the God of your fathers,
increase you a thousand-fold more than you are
and bless you, just as He has promised you!"*
Deuteronomy 1:10–11

*D*ear Heavenly Father, let my trust in You never waver. Give me wisdom and courage for this day.

MARCH 27

It was at this time that He went off
to the mountain to pray, and He spent
the whole night in prayer to God.
And when day came, He called His disciples to Him
and chose twelve of them,
whom He also named as apostles.
Luke 6:12–13

Christ prayed all night for the men who would preach, teach, heal the sick, raise the dead, and record His Words. When it's time to do battle, we need to be alone first.

MARCH 28

A father of the fatherless and a judge for the widows,
Is God in His holy habitation.
Psalm 68:5

God has promised to be "a father to the fatherless." If you're a single mom, count on Him to keep His Word. And instead of attempting to be both father and mother, you can just be a mom to your kids. Lord, help me to entrust all my heavy burdens to Your care.

MARCH 29

"Hear, O Israel! The LORD is our God,
the LORD is one!"
Deuteronomy 6:4

*T*hroughout the scriptures there are references to the contributions of the Triune God. While the Father spoke from heaven, confirming Christ at His baptism, the Holy Spirit descended upon Christ as a dove. Only God could have omnisciently conceived of the Trinity. God has always been, and will forever be.

MARCH 30

And He called the twelve together,
and gave them power and authority
over all the demons and to heal diseases.
And He sent them out to proclaim
the kingdom of God and to perform healing.
Luke 9:1–2

*L*ord, how grateful I am that Your Holy Spirit worked in the lives of these apostles, molding them into strong men of faith. Help me to become unselfish with my time so that many more will hear the gospel.

MARCH 31

"When you enter the land which the LORD
your God gives you, you shall not learn to imitate
the detestable things of those nations. . . .
For whoever does these things is detestable to the LORD;
and because of these detestable things
the LORD your God will drive them out before you.
Deuteronomy 18:9, 12

*I*s God receiving all the glory in your life? Lord, You know better than I what things will draw my time and attention away from You. Give me the courage to obey You.

APRIL 1

And behold, two men were talking with Him;
and they were Moses and Elijah, who,
appearing in glory, were speaking
of His departure which He
was about to accomplish at Jerusalem.
Luke 9:30–31

*I*n case you've been feeling sorry for Moses who never got to enter the Promised Land, just look at what God had in store for him. Oh Lord, I am so grateful that our place with You is already reserved!

APRIL 2

Be to me a rock of habitation,
to which I may continually come;
You have given commandment to save me,
For You are my rock and my fortress.
Psalm 71:3

Over fifty times in scripture, the word *rock* is used in reference to God. When everything else fails, He is steadfast, immovable, and unchangeable.

APRIL 3

"But it shall come about, if you do
not obey the LORD your God,
to observe to do all His commandments
and His statutes with which I charge you today,
that all these curses will come
upon you and overtake you."
Deuteronomy 28:15

Lord, the people of Noah's day refused to heed his preaching. Help me to be a better witness before time again runs out.

APRIL 4

A woman named Martha welcomed Him
into her home. She had a sister
called Mary, who was seated at the Lord's feet,
listening to His word.
But Martha was distracted with
all her preparations; and she came up
to Him and said, "Lord, do You not
care that my sister has left me
to do all the serving alone?"
Luke 10:38–40

*H*ave you taken time to get to know your Lord? Perhaps your life, like Martha's, is missing the best part.

APRIL 5

"Moreover the LORD your God will
circumcise your heart and the heart
of your descendants, to love the LORD
your God with all your heart and
with all your soul, so that you may live."
Deuteronomy 30:6

*F*ather, I know circumcision of my heart is wrought by Your Holy Spirit. Lord, make me willing to undergo transformation that I might truly love both You and others.

APRIL 6

Listen, O my people, to my instruction;
Incline your ears to the words of my mouth.
I will open my mouth in a parable;
I will utter dark sayings of old,
Which we have heard and known,
And our fathers have told us.
Psalm 78:1–3

When you examine the contents of my heart, Lord, which type of soil have I prepared for Your Word?

APRIL 7

Then Moses called to Joshua and said
to him in the sight of all Israel,
"Be strong and courageous, for you shall go
with this people into the land which
the LORD has sworn to their fathers
to give them, and you shall give it
to them as an inheritance."
Deuteronomy 31:7

Lord, I forget sometimes that those in leadership are chosen by You. And with responsibility comes accountability.

APRIL 8

"And I say to you, everyone who confesses
Me before men, the Son of Man will confess
him also before the angels of God; but he who
denies Me before men will be denied
before the angels of God."
Luke 12:8–9

*E*veryone is in need of a Savior. The Bible states clearly that only one person fills this job description. "And there is salvation in no one else" (Acts 4:12). Jesus Christ is that Savior.

APRIL 9

He who withholds his rod hates his son,
But he who loves him disciplines him diligently.
Proverbs 13:24

*D*iscipline is meant to teach the correct behavior. "Punishment" only makes a child bitter. Lord, help me to remember what Anne Ortlund teaches, that children are like wet cement. Assist me in making good impressions in their lives.

APRIL 10

"O Jerusalem, Jerusalem, you who
kill the prophets and stone those sent to you,
how often I have longed to gather your
children together, as a hen gathers her
chicks under her wings, but you were not willing!"
Luke 13:34 NIV

*H*ow like the Israelites I am! God showed them the path they were to walk in, yet time after time they leaped beyond the lines of safety and tried to live without Him. Is it time for you to let God steer the course?

APRIL 11

Now Joshua the son of Nun was filled
with the spirit of wisdom, for Moses
had laid his hands on him; and the sons
of Israel listened to him and did
as the LORD *had commanded Moses.*
Deuteronomy 34:9

*F*ather, as you did with Joshua, lead me to new heights in my walk with You.

APRIL 12

Help us, O God of our salvation,
for the glory of Your name;
And deliver us and forgive our sins
for Your name's sake.
Psalm 79:9

We thank You that we can come to You as Lord and Messiah. You are truly a God of forgiveness.

APRIL 13

With cunning they conspire against
your people; they plot against those you cherish.
"Come," they say, "let us destroy them as a nation,
that the name of Israel be
remembered no more."
Psalm 83:3–4 NIV

Even in King David's time the survival of the Jews appeared precarious at best. God spared and preserved David from invading armies, despite all odds, and used him to raise up a nation. Lord, today Your power still sustains the Jews. Give them true faith!

APRIL 14

Then Joshua the son of Nun sent two
men as spies secretly from Shittim, saying,
"Go, view the land, especially Jericho."
So they went and came into the house
of a harlot whose name was Rahab, and lodged there.
Joshua 2:1

Lord, Rahab believed You and You used her to hide Joshua's spies. How can You use me?

APRIL 15

Every person is to be in subjection to the
governing authorities. For there is no
authority except from God, and those
which exist are established by God. . . .
For because of this you also pay taxes,
for rulers are servants of God, devoting
themselves to this very thing.
Romans 13:1, 6

Lord, let me give to the government not grudgingly but out of obedience to You. And please assist those in authority over me to direct wisely the use of these funds.

APRIL 16

"Or what woman, if she has ten silver coins
and loses one coin, does not light a lamp and
sweep the house and search carefully until she finds it?
When she has found it, she calls together her
friends and neighbors, saying,
'Rejoice with me.'"
Luke 15:8–9

Jesus compared the woman's joy to the celebration that goes on in heaven when a sinner repents and "Sonbeams" of peace finally flood the soul. It's the feeling of "wholeness" a person hungers for all her life.

APRIL 17

And a poor man named Lazarus was
laid at his gate, covered with sores. . . .
Now the poor man died
and was carried away by the angels
to Abraham's bosom.
Luke 16:20, 22

Once life has ceased, we no longer have the power to change our eternal destination. Although he suffered in life, the poor man now resided in paradise.

APRIL 18

"Take up for yourselves twelve stones from
here out of the middle of the Jordan,
from the place where the priests' feet
are standing firm, and carry them over
with you, and lay them down in the lodging
place where you will lodge tonight."
Joshua 4:3

Lord, please pave my way with stones from You, stones of dedication, perseverance, and compassion.

APRIL 19

And they were bringing children to Him so that
He might touch them; but the disciples rebuked them.
But when Jesus saw this, He was indignant
and said to them, "Permit the children to come to Me;
do not hinder them; for the kingdom of
God belongs to such as these. Truly I say to you,
whoever does not receive the kingdom of
God like a child will not enter it at all."
Mark 10:13–15

Lord, only You can offer true comfort to those who have lost little ones.

APRIL 20

The LORD said to Joshua,
"See, I have given Jericho into your hand,
with its king and the valiant warriors.
You shall march around the city,
all the men of war circling the city once.
You shall do so for six days."
Joshua 6:2–3

*L*ord, I need to remember that You're the Lord who not only guarantees victory in the battle, but draws up the winning strategy. Thank You for that assurance.

APRIL 21

"Be on your guard! If your brother sins,
rebuke him; and if he repents, forgive him."
Luke 17:3

*H*ere Jesus admonished his disciples to "rebuke" their brothers if they've sinned. Why? Because sin is a progressive fall. And "real love" means intervening that they might get back on track.

APRIL 22

How lovely are Your dwelling places,
O LORD of hosts! My soul longed and
even yearned for the courts of the LORD;
My heart and my flesh sing for joy to the living God.
Psalm 84:1–2

*H*ow King David must have longed for a lasting peace. But he had to settle for that little niche of peace he carved out for himself while pondering what heaven was like, anticipating the day he'd dwell with God.

APRIL 23

Then He took the twelve aside
and said to them, "Behold, we are going
up to Jerusalem, and all things which
are written through the prophets about
the Son of Man will be accomplished.
For He will be handed over to the Gentiles,
and will be mocked and mistreated
and spit upon, and after they have scourged
Him, they will kill Him; and the third day
He will rise again."
Luke 18:31–33

*F*ather, help me realize, like the disciples, that You are always with me, to the end.

APRIL 24

Then Joshua spoke to the LORD. . .
in the sight of Israel, "O sun, stand still at Gibeon,
And O moon in the valley of Aijalon."
So the sun stood still, and the moon stopped,
Until the nation avenged themselves
of their enemies.
Joshua 10:12–13

If God is able to stop the solar system, He is able to deal with every crisis in your life.

APRIL 25

"In a certain city there was a judge who
did not fear God and did not respect man.
There was a widow in that city,
and she kept coming to him, saying,
'Give me legal protection from my opponent.'"
Luke 18:2–5

Lord, You alone judge rightly. You alone will administer to the guilty the punishment they truly deserve.

APRIL 26

A wise son accepts his father's discipline,
But a scoffer does not listen to rebuke.
From the fruit of a man's mouth he enjoys good,
But the desire of the treacherous is violence.
The one who guards his mouth preserves his life;
The one who opens wide his lips comes to ruin.
Proverbs 13:1–3

*E*ach day presents an opportunity to extend to others words that reach in to soothe and heal souls—or deepen wounds.

APRIL 27

There is no one like You among the gods, O LORD;
Nor are there any works like Yours. . . .
For You are great and do wondrous deeds;
You alone are God.
Psalm 86:8, 10

*L*ord, You've given me an entire Bible to read so that I might learn of Your love, concern, and compassion. Develop in me that sensitivity to "hear the prompting of Your Spirit" while You guide me toward the truth.

APRIL 28

Now these are the territories which the sons
of Israel inherited in the land of Canaan,
which Eleazar the priest, and Joshua the son of Nun,
and the heads of the households of the tribes
of the sons of Israel apportioned
to them for an inheritance, by the lot
of their inheritance, as the LORD
commanded through Moses.
Joshua 14:1–2

Lord, I know that all things work to bring about Your plan. Please continue to protect Your chosen people.

APRIL 29

"Go into the village ahead of you
there as you enter, you will find a colt tied
on which no one yet has ever sat; untie it
and bring it here. If anyone asks you,
'Why are you untying it?' you shall say,
'The Lord has need of it.'"
Luke 19:30–31

Lord, thank You for all the "absolutes" of scripture. I believe You are exactly who You claim to be, God Incarnate.

APRIL 30

*Now it came about after the death
of Joshua that the sons of Israel inquired
of the LORD, saying, "Who shall go
up first for us against the Canaanites,
to fight against them?"*
Judges 1:1–2

*I*srael thought they could peacefully coexist with idol worshipers, but little by little they allowed this sea of sin to seep into the undergirding of their own society. When we move away from God's will, all manner of sin can somehow be justified.

MAY 1

*In the beginning was the Word,
and the Word was with God,
and the Word was God. He
was in the beginning with God.*
John 1:1–2

*Th*e apostle John was an eyewitness to the events he was inspired by God's Spirit to record for us. "By this you know the Spirit of God: every spirit that confesses that Jesus Christ has come in the flesh is from God" (1 John 4:2).

MAY 2

It is good to give thanks to the LORD,
And to sing praises to Your name, O Most High;
To declare Your lovingkindness in the morning
And Your faithfulness by night.
Psalm 92:1–2

Lord, thank You for music and the way it uplifts my spirits. No matter what time of day or season, I rejoice in worshiping You.

MAY 3

The wise woman builds her house,
But the foolish tears it down
with her own hands.
Proverbs 14:1

Every woman must understand God's "building codes" in order to strengthen her own household. Lord, You are the Master Builder. To stay upright I must follow Your blueprints.

MAY 4

And the Word became flesh,
and dwelt among us, and we saw His glory,
glory as of the only begotten from the Father,
full of grace and truth.
John 1:14

*I*t's our nature to sin. That's why we need a new nature. This is exactly what Christ purchased for us on Calvary's cross, the right to be indwelt with the very Spirit of God. A fresh start, isn't that what all of us are seeking?

MAY 5

"I brought you up out of Egypt
and led you into the land which
I have sworn to your fathers; and I said,
'I will never break My covenant with you,
and as for you, you shall make no covenant
with the inhabitants of this land;
you shall tear down their altars.'
But you have not obeyed Me."
Judges 2:1–2

*L*ord, cleanse my soul and fill me with Your strength that I might not backslide into the pit of disobedience again.

MAY 6

Wisdom reposes in the heart of the discerning
and even among fools she lets herself be known.
Proverbs 14:33 NIV

*A*lthough we can't change others' hearts, our own can be filled with wisdom. Confident in our eternal destination, we can exude serenity, peace, and love.

MAY 7

Now the sons of Israel again
did evil in the sight of the LORD.
So the LORD strengthened Eglon
the king of Moab against Israel,
because they had done evil in the sight of the LORD. . . .
The sons of Israel served Eglon
the king of Moab eighteen years.
Judges 3:12–14

*L*ord, please instill in me a hunger for daily study and worship, that I might not sin.

MAY 8

They asked, and He brought quail,
and satisfied them
with the bread of heaven.
Psalm 105:40

*L*ord, I long for the living bread. I long to live forever in Your glorious presence.

MAY 9

They asked him,
"What then? Are you Elijah?"
And he said, "I am not."
John 1:21

*F*ather, both Jesus and John the Baptist delivered the truth of Your Word, but people refused to heed their messages. Lord, help me to listen and respond.

MAY 10

The plans of the heart belong to man,
But the answer of the tongue is from the LORD.
All the ways of a man are clean in his own sight,
But the LORD weighs the motives.
Commit your works to the LORD,
And your plans will be established.
Proverbs 16:1–3

*L*ord, there have been times when I compromised the Truth of Your Word. Please help me get back on track. Place my feet firmly on the pavement of Your Word.

MAY 11

Now Deborah, a prophetess,
the wife of Lappidoth, was judging Israel at that time.
She used to sit under the palm tree
of Deborah between Ramah and Bethel
in the hill country of Ephraim;
and the sons of Israel came
up to her for judgment.
Judges 4:4–5

*L*ord, thank You for using a woman to save Israel!

MAY 12

"Arise! For this is the day
in which the LORD *has given Sisera*
into your hands;
behold, the LORD *has gone out before you."*
Judges 4:14

*G*od began to display His awesome power. A great storm arose, and the rain and hail pelted the faces of Sisera's troops, rendering vision impossible. Israel, with their backs to the storm, began to attack. Meanwhile, Sisera fled on foot and was killed by a woman. Deborah's prophecy had come true.

MAY 13

His name will be
called Wonderful Counselor,
Mighty God, Eternal Father,
Prince of Peace.
Isaiah 9:6

*F*ather, I thank You that I can call You many names, and all of them are beautiful and holy.

MAY 14

He found first his own brother Simon
and said to him,
"We have found the Messiah"
(which translated means Christ).
John 1:41

*H*ow blessed for Andrew that his brother responded and they shared the love of the Lord together. Lord, I pray for strength to share Your love with unbelieving family members.

MAY 15

The stone which the builders
rejected has become
the chief corner stone.
Psalm 118:22

*W*hen a building is started, a cornerstone must be placed precisely, because the rest of the structure is lined up with it. Lord Jesus Christ, You alone are to be the cornerstone of my life. Please help me to discard those concerns that block my view of You.

MAY 16

The LORD will tear down
the house of the proud,
But He will establish
the boundary of the widow.
Proverbs 15:25

*F*ather, let me share Your Word with those women who now find themselves alone—"Now she who is a widow indeed and who has been left alone, has fixed her hope on God and continues in entreaties and prayers night and day" (1 Timothy 5:5).

MAY 17

Gideon was beating out wheat
in the wine press in order
to save it from the Midianites.
The angel of the LORD appeared
to him and said to him, "The LORD is with you,
O valiant warrior."
Judges 6:11–12

*H*ave you ever felt that the weight of the world rested on your shoulders? Well, that's Gideon for you. The Lord gave Gideon the same resounding message of assurance which He always gives to His servants: that He was with Him and that was enough.

MAY 18

When the wine ran out,
the mother of Jesus said to Him,
"They have no wine."
John 2:3

*F*ather, You are still the God of miracles. I thank You that You know my needs.

MAY 19

I have told of my ways,
and You have answered me;
Teach me Your statutes.
Make me understand the way of Your precepts,
So I will meditate on Your wonders.
Psalm 119:26–27

*L*ord, teach me Your ways, that I might live out Your precepts before my family and loved ones.

MAY 20

When a wicked man comes,
contempt also comes,
And with dishonor comes scorn.
Proverbs 18:3

*W*omen become vulnerable the instant truth is replaced with desire. It's like when the tip of an arrow finds the one small point of vulnerability and penetrates a suit of armor. Lord, sometimes I want so badly to be loved that I trust the wrong people. Please guide me to those who are trustworthy.

MAY 21

Jesus answered and said to him,
"Truly, truly, I say to you,
unless one is born again
he cannot see the kingdom of God."
John 3:3

*L*ord, You told Nicodemus he must be born again. I praise You that You are the God of second chances, the God of truth!

MAY 22

And the LORD said to Gideon,
"The people who are with you are too many
for Me to give Midian into their hands,
for Israel would become boastful, saying,
'My own power has delivered me.'
Now therefore come, proclaim
in the hearing of the people,
saying, 'Whoever is afraid and trembling,
let him return and depart from Mount Gilead.'"
So 22,000 people returned, but 10,000 remained.
Judges 7:2–3

*I*f God is on our side, we don't need anyone else.

MAY 23

Your eyes have seen my unformed substance;
And in Your book were all written,
The days that were ordained for me,
When as yet there was not one of them.
Psalm 139:16

*G*od has a definite purpose for your life. He wants to use your life to further His kingdom. And if you are in His will, the last page will have a very happy ending!

MAY 24

An excellent wife, who can find?
For her worth is far above jewels.
The heart of her husband trusts in her,
And he will have no lack of gain.
She does him good and not evil
All the days of her life.
Proverbs 31:10–12

*L*ord, forgive my selfish tendencies and show me the path to virtue.

MAY 25

"He who believes in the Son has eternal life;
but he who does not obey the Son
will not see life,
but the wrath of God abides on him."
John 3:36

*T*he Word of God says that we can have absolute assurance of eternal life today. As we grasp that truth, our lives are transformed.

MAY 26

"Speak, now, in the hearing of all the leaders of
Shechem, 'Which is better for you, that seventy men,
all the sons of Jerubbaal, rule over you,
or that one man rule over you?'
Also, remember that I am your bone and your flesh."
Judges 9:1–2

*T*he God of justice always intervenes to bring the course
of history in line with His own design. Lord, Your eyes see
everything. You are a God of unswerving justice.

MAY 27

Praise the LORD! Praise God in His sanctuary;
Praise Him in His mighty expanse.
Praise Him for His mighty deeds;
Praise Him according to His excellent greatness. . . .
Let everything that has breath praise the LORD.
Praise the LORD!
Psalm 150:1–2, 6

*I*n other words, "Praise Him with all you've got to make
noise with!" Isn't that what true worship is, using our entire
beings to give Him the glory He deserves?

MAY 28

So He came to a city of Samaria called Sychar,
near the parcel of ground that Jacob
gave to his son Joseph; and Jacob's well was there.
So Jesus, being wearied from His journey,
was sitting thus by the well.
It was about the sixth hour.
There came a woman of Samaria to draw water.
Jesus said to her, "Give Me a drink."
John 4:5–7

*L*ord, help me to seek out those who, for whatever reason, are shunned and despised. They need You so much.

MAY 29

Then it shall be that whatever
comes out of the doors of my house
to meet me when I return in peace from the
sons of Ammon, it shall be the LORD's,
and I will offer it up as a burnt offering. . . .
When Jephthah came to his house at Mizpah,
behold, his daughter was coming out to meet
him with tambourines and with dancing.
Judges 11:31, 34

*L*ord, help me turn to You for my deliverance and not make hasty, costly vows.

MAY 30

The words of the Preacher,
the son of David, king in Jerusalem.
"Vanity of vanities," says the Preacher,
"Vanity of vanities! All is vanity."
Ecclesiastes 1:1–2

Solomon had experienced the best the world had to offer. . .and it wasn't enough. Lord, please help me view my
priorities from Your perspective.

MAY 31

Now there is in Jerusalem by the sheep gate a pool. . .
having five porticoes. In these lay a multitude
of those who were sick, blind, lame, and withered,
[waiting for the moving of the waters. . .
whoever then first, after the stirring up of the water,
stepped in was made well.]
John 5:2–4

Lord, if sin is at the root of my infirmity, then bring
me to swift repentance. But if my suffering is to point others toward Your glory, quench my thirst with Your living
water.

JUNE 1

*Now Ibzan of Bethlehem judged Israel
after him. He had thirty sons,
and thirty daughters whom he gave
in marriage outside the family,
and he brought in thirty daughters
from outside for his sons.*
Judges 12:8–9

What other tangible effects of his presence on earth did this judge of Israel leave behind? How can we discern the will of God for our lives? Daily prayer is definitely the main source, not only relating our needs to God, but also listening for His directions.

JUNE 2

*I said to myself, "Come now,
I will test you with pleasure.
So enjoy yourself." And behold, it too was futility.
I said of laughter, "It is madness," and of pleasure,
"What does it accomplish?"*
Ecclesiastes 2:1–2

Lord, help me not to be drawn away from You by the endless pursuit of things. Instead, I desire Your presence, guidance, and wisdom.

JUNE 3

"As the living Father sent Me,
and I live because of the Father
so he who eats Me, he also will live because of Me.
This is the bread which came down out of heaven;
not as the fathers ate and died;
he who eats this bread will live forever."
John 6:57–58

To truly partake of Christ is to accept Him as He is, fully God and fully man. He was sent from God, who recognized our need for Him.

JUNE 4

Then the angel of the LORD appeared to the woman
and said to her, "Behold now, you are barren
and have borne no children,
but you shall conceive and give birth to a son."
Judges 13:3

Once again, God was about to raise up a deliverer for Israel. Lord, as I read Your Word, open my eyes to Your infinite wisdom and understanding.

JUNE 5

When the sons of Ammon
fought against Israel, the elders of Gilead
went to get Jephthah from the land of Tob.
Judges 11:5

*A*s women, it's up to us to uphold the sanctity of life. Each life comes into this world with a purpose. Therefore, when that life is abruptly ended, so are all the accomplishments that were intended for that unique person. Lord, give me words to describe Your greatest gift—life.

JUNE 6

Now the feast of the Jews,
the Feast of Booths, was near.
Therefore His brothers said to Him,
"Leave here, and go into Judea,
so that Your disciples also may see Your
works which You are doing. . . ."
For not even His brothers
were believing in Him.
John 7:2–5

*T*hank You, Jesus, for reminding me to wait for God's timing in my life, especially when the pressure applied by others would have me rush on ahead.

JUNE 7

Then the woman gave birth to
a son and named him Samson;
and the child grew up and the LORD blessed him.
Judges 13:24

As Samson struck out on his own, the first thing he did was fall in love with a Philistine woman. Although his parents cautioned him against marrying a pagan, he was determined. Samson's misuse of power caused the Philistines to kill his bride and her father. Lord, I pray for discernment in my own life that I may prosper and not selfishly hurt others.

JUNE 8

There is an appointed time for everything.
And there is a time for every event under heaven. . . .
A time to weep and a time to laugh;
A time to mourn and a time to dance.
Ecclesiastes 3:1, 4

Once we've finally accepted that God truly loves us, it's hard to face the first discouraging episode of tragedy that follows. Lord, through my veil of tears help me to view Your rescuing hand, that I might reach out to grasp You more firmly.

JUNE 9

The scribes and the Pharisees brought
a woman caught in adultery,
and having set her in the center of the court,
they said to Him,
"Teacher, this woman has been caught in adultery,
in the very act. Now in the Law Moses
commanded us to stone such women;
what then do You say?"
John 8:3–5

Lord, forgive me, no matter what my sin, that I might turn from it and faithfully serve You.

JUNE 10

Now Samson lay until midnight,
and at midnight he arose and took hold
of the doors of the city gate and the
two posts and pulled them up along with the bars. . . .
After this it came about that he loved a
woman in the valley of Sorek,
whose name was Delilah.
Judges 16:3–4

Lord, give me the gift of discernment that my life may be a consistent testimony of my love for You.

June 11

Remember also your Creator
in the days of your youth,
before the evil days come and the years
draw near when you will say,
"I have no delight in them." . . .
Fear God and keep His commandments,
because this applies to every person.
Ecclesiastes 12:1, 13

Have you forgotten the God of your youth? Have His principles been compromised away by the pressures of a world that teaches the Ten Commandments are optional? With the Lord's help, it's not too late to turn it all around.

June 12

As He passed by, He saw a man blind from birth.
And His disciples asked Him,
"Rabbi, who sinned, this man or his parents,
that he would be born blind?" Jesus answered,
"It was neither. . .but it was so
that the works of God might be displayed."
John 9:1–3

Rather than believe that this man had been healed, the Pharisees donned their masks of spiritual blindness. No miracle of God was about to shake up their world! Lord, open my eyes to Your miracles.

JUNE 13

Then Elimelech, Naomi's husband, died;
and she was left with her two sons.
They took for themselves Moabite
women as wives; the name of the one was
Orpah and the name of the other Ruth.
Ruth 1:3–4

*F*ew daughters-in-law would have persisted in devotion to a woman whose life held such abysmal tragedy and so little prospect for change. However, God had a glorious plan. Ruth would become Boaz's bride and mother to his son, whose lineage would include the Messiah, Jesus Christ.

JUNE 14

She, greatly distressed, prayed to the Lord
and wept bitterly. She made a vow and said,
"O Lord of hosts, if You will indeed look
on the affliction of Your maidservant and
remember me, and not forget Your maidservant,
but will give Your maidservant a son,
then I will give him to the Lord
all the days of his life."
1 Samuel 1:10–11

*T*he persistent prayers of a Christian woman should never be underestimated!

JUNE 15

"My beloved responded and said to me,
'Arise, my darling, my beautiful one,
And come along. For behold, the winter is past,
The rain is over and gone. The flowers have
already appeared in the land;
The time has arrived for pruning the vines,
And the voice of the turtledove
has been heard in our land. . . .
Arise, my darling, my beautiful one,
And come along!'"
Song of Solomon 2:10–13

Lord, make me a woman who is faithfully devoted to You.

JUNE 16

"But he who enters by the door is a shepherd of the sheep.
To him the doorkeeper opens,
and the sheep hear his voice,
and he calls his own sheep by name
and leads them out."
John 10:2–3

God calls us by name, just as the shepherd has pet names for his sheep. Someday, when the King of kings, our Good Shepherd, calls us home to heaven, we'll hear the name He calls us.

June 17

*It came about in due time,
after Hannah had conceived,
that she gave birth to a son;
and she named him Samuel, saying,
"Because I have asked him of the Lord."*
1 Samuel 1:20

Lord, if You should give me a child, guide me as You guided Hannah—to sincere faithfulness.

June 18

*The vision of Isaiah the son of Amoz
concerning Judah and Jerusalem. . . .
Listen, O heavens, and hear, O earth;
For the Lord speaks, "Sons I have reared
and brought up, but they have revolted against Me. . . .
My people do not understand."*
Isaiah 1:1–3

Lord, this book displays Your promises and prophecies. Open my mind to receive Your truth. And keep me from confusion, that I might know You as both Messiah and Lord.

JUNE 19

Now a certain man was sick,
Lazarus of Bethany. . . .
So the sisters sent word to Him, saying,
"Lord, behold, he whom You love is sick."
John 11:1, 3

*H*ave you allowed Christ to exercise His authority to bring you forth to new life? Lord, strengthen my faith so that when tragedy strikes, I know that You are the Resurrection and the Life.

JUNE 20

Then Hannah prayed and said,
"My heart exults in the LORD;
My horn is exalted in the LORD. . . .
There is no one holy like the LORD,
Indeed, there is no one besides You,
Nor is there any rock like our God."
1 Samuel 2:1–2

*H*annah spent her time in the temple, praying and serving others. God granted the deepest longing of her heart, despite the fact that she was just a sinner who could offer God nothing but her brokenness and yielded spirit.

JUNE 21

Unless the LORD of hosts had left us a few survivors,
We would be like Sodom,
We would be like Gomorrah. . . .
Hear the word of the LORD, you rulers of Sodom;
Give ear to the instruction of our God,
you people of Gomorrah.
Isaiah 1:9–10

*L*ord, thank You for sending Your messengers to minister to my heart. Through them the light of Your truth finally dawned in my heart. Thank You for Your peace.

JUNE 22

Mary then a pound of very costly perfume
of pure nard, and anointed the feet of Jesus
and wiped His feet with her hair;
and the house was filled
with the fragrance of the perfume.
John 12:3

*L*ord, let me never take You for granted.

JUNE 23

"Thus says the LORD, 'Did I not indeed
reveal Myself to the house of your father
when they were in Egypt in bondage to Pharaoh's
house? Did I not choose them from
all the tribes of Israel to be My priests. . . ?
Why do you kick at My sacrifice
and at My offering which I have commanded
in My dwelling, and honor your sons above Me?'"
1 Samuel 2:27–29

Lord, instill obedience in me also.

JUNE 24

For You have abandoned Your people,
the house of Jacob, because they are filled
with influences from the east,
And they are soothsayers like the Philistines,
And they strike bargains with the children of foreigners.
. . . Their land has also been filled with idols;
They worship the work of their hands,
That which their fingers have made.
Isaiah 2:6–8

Lord, be in charge of my own priority list.

JUNE 25

"He who believes in Me, does not believe in Me
but in Him who sent Me. He who sees Me
sees the One who sent Me. I have come
as Light into the world, so that everyone who believes in
Me will not remain in darkness."
John 12:44–46

Your truth is readily available, Lord. Therefore, I know with certainty that I will one day see You face-to-face. Deepen my faith so that I might penetrate the spiritual darkness around me.

JUNE 26

The LORD called Samuel; and he said,
"Here I am."
1 Samuel 3:4

Lord, keep me close to You, that I may always hear You.

JUNE 27

"Therefore the Lord Himself will give you a sign:
Behold, a virgin will be with child and bear a son,
and she will call His name Immanuel."
Isaiah 7:14

This prediction of Christ's conception was delivered over 700 years before He was actually born. In announcing to Joseph that Mary was with child by the power of God's Spirit, the angel used these exact words from Isaiah. Lord, thank You that what You have said always comes to pass.

JUNE 28

Jesus, knowing that the Father had given
all things into His hands, and that He
had come forth from God, and was going back to God,
got up from supper, and laid aside His garments;
and taking a towel, He girded Himself.
John 13:3–4

How difficult it must have been for Christ to say good-bye to his disciples, knowing they still didn't fully comprehend His impending death! So Jesus set about to love them and to show them that they were likewise called to be servants.

JUNE 29

*The oracle concerning Babylon which Isaiah
the son of Amoz saw. Lift up a standard on the
bare hill, raise your voice to them. . . .
Wail, for the day of the LORD is near!
It will come as destruction from the Almighty.*
Isaiah 13:1–2, 6

*T*here is a specific time in history when the final judgment against the disobedient will take place. Lord, thank You for Your Word which contains not only the promise of salvation, but the promise of judgment.

JUNE 30

*"In My Father's house are many dwelling places;
if it were not so, I would have told you;
for I go to prepare a place for you."*
John 14:2

*J*esus Christ has promised to prepare a place for us in heaven. The only problem is that we have to wait down here until He's got our mansion ready for us. Lord, thank You for the Holy Spirit, who brings us peace and comfort until we can be united with You in heaven.

JULY 1

So the Philistines fought and Israel
was defeated, and every man fled to his tent,
and the slaughter was very great. . . .
And the ark of God was taken.
1 Samuel 4:10–11

As long as the Israelites kept the ark of God with them, they were invincible to the nations which sought to conquer them, for the Lord's presence was among them. Because they had forsaken God, He was about to teach them what life would be like without Him on their side.

JULY 2

And it came about when Samuel
was old that he appointed his sons judges over Israel. . . .
His sons, however, did not walk in his ways.
1 Samuel 8:1, 3

Seeing the wickedness of Samuel's sons, the elders of Israel asked for a human king, so they might be "like all the nations." But they'd always been the envy of these other nations, which knew that Israel's king was God Almighty. Lord, give me insight to make You king of my life.

JULY 3

*"As the branch cannot bear fruit of itself
unless it abides in the vine, so neither can you
unless you abide in Me. I am the vine,
you are the branches; he who abides in Me
and I in him, he bears much fruit;
for apart from Me you can do nothing."*
John 15:4–5

The same offer to abide in the vine is extended to all who hear the gospel message. Have you responded? How diligently are you abiding?

JULY 4

*"Then the glory of the LORD will be revealed,
And all flesh will see it together;
For the mouth of the LORD has spoken."*
Isaiah 40:5

Only when we are totally dependent on our Redeemer are we truly free! Lord Jesus, I rejoice that You came to be my Redeemer. Hallelujah! Amen!

JULY 5

The nations will see your righteousness,
And all kings your glory;
And you will be called by a new name,
Which the mouth of the LORD will designate.
Isaiah 62:2

Whenever God sets about to perform a work of regeneration, He also provides a new name. Lord, my name remains the same, but my heart is forever changed by Your love.

JULY 6

"It is to your advantage that I go away;
for if I do not go away,
the Helper will not come to you;
but if I go, I will send Him to you."
John 16:7

The Holy Spirit was presented to the disciples as a tongue of fire, that they might have proof of His appearance. He would be with them every moment to guide, and to convict the world concerning sin, righteousness, and judgment. Are you aware of these things in your own life?

JULY 7

He had a son whose name was Saul,
a choice and handsome man,
and there was not a more handsome person
than he among the sons of Israel;
from his shoulders and up
he was taller than any of the people.
1 Samuel 9:2

Outward appearance means nothing if that person isn't fully committed to God. God chose Saul to be Israel's king so that this nation might eventually learn their need for spiritual discernment.

JULY 8

Thus says the LORD, "Heaven is My throne
and the earth is My footstool.
Where then is a house you could build for Me?
And where is a place that I may rest?"
Isaiah 66:1

The temple was the earthly place that God established for worship, so that people could fellowship together in praise of our Creator. However, true worship begins in our hearts. Jesus Christ is not only our Creator, but He is the head of the Church and the world is His footstool.

JULY 9

*"This is eternal life, that they may know You
the only true God, and Jesus Christ
whom You have sent."*
John 17:3

*H*ave you ever unwittingly overheard an intimate conversation? Well, that's exactly what this chapter of John is like. We are privileged to overhear Jesus as He speaks to the Father. His prayer includes concern for those whom the Father has given to Him. He prayed that God's power would keep us from being swayed by the world and the evil one.

JULY 10

*"About this time tomorrow I will send you a man
from the land of Benjamin, and you shall anoint him
to be prince over My people Israel;
and he will deliver My people
from the hand of the Philistines.
For I have regarded My people,
because their cry has come to Me."*
1 Samuel 9:16

*L*ord, help me trust in Your strength to instill, infuse, and instruct so that I serve You obediently.

JULY 11

Now the word of the LORD came to me saying,
"Before I formed you in the womb I knew you,
And before you were born I consecrated you;
I have appointed you a prophet to the nations."
Jeremiah 1:4–5

*L*ord, I pray for answers to the dilemmas which plague our society. Not knowing whom You have called for special service, let me respect and revere each life with hope, anticipation, and gratitude.

JULY 12

When Jesus had spoken these words,
He went forth with His disciples
over the ravine of the Kidron,
where there was a garden,
which He entered with His disciples.
Now Judas also, who was betraying Him,
knew the place.
John 18:1–2

*W*hat could possibly be worse than being betrayed? Having the one who is disloyal rise up from among those who called you friend! Lord, make straight my wavering path! Help me abide in Your truth.

JULY 13

"Fill your horn with oil and go;
I will send you to Jesse the Bethlehemite,
for I have selected a king for Myself
among his sons."
1 Samuel 16:1

Saul had been summoned by the Lord for service as king. Yet Saul had relied on his own strength, and it failed him. This character flaw eventually brought him down to complete disgrace, and the Lord chose another king. Lord, keep me from misusing the power and authority You give me.

JULY 14

"They will fight against you,
but they will not overcome you,
for I am with you to deliver you,"
declares the LORD.
Jeremiah 1:19

We humans are resilient, able to withstand almost any hardship as long as we know we're not abandoned. God always provides a way through, for Israel and for us.

JULY 15

*Jesus answered him, "I have spoken openly
to the world; I always taught in synagogues
and in the temple, where all the Jews come together;
and I spoke nothing in secret.
Why do you question Me?
Question those who have heard
what I spoke to them;
they know what I said."*
John 18:20–21

Lord, break down my walls of stubbornness which prevent me from hearing, seeing, and rallying to Your message.

JULY 16

*Then David spoke to the men who
were standing by him, saying,
" Who is this uncircumcised Philistine,
that he should taunt the armies of the living God?"*
1 Samuel 17:26

David refused to allow Goliath's attitude to stand unchallenged. His victory came by the power of the Lord, not by man's might. Lord, remind me of this when I face my own "giants."

JULY 17

"At that time they will call Jerusalem
'The Throne of the LORD,' and all the nations
will be gathered to it, to Jerusalem,
for the name of the LORD;
nor will they walk anymore after
the stubbornness of their evil heart."
Jeremiah 3:17

True peace will reign in Israel when Christ returns again to earth (Matthew 24:29–39). Lord, help me wait!

JULY 18

Pilate wrote an inscription
and put it on the cross.
It was written, "JESUS THE NAZARENE,
THE KING OF THE JEWS."
John 19:19

God overruled the Jews' request when Pilate refused to change the sign on the cross. Pilate knew Christ was exactly who He claimed to be, King of the Jews, the promised Messiah. Yet Pilate lacked the gumption to stand by his conviction. Lord, give me the courage to stand firmly in my convictions.

JULY 19

*"The LORD therefore be judge
and decide between you and me;
and may He see and plead my cause
and deliver me from your hand."*
1 Samuel 24:15

Saul had pursued David relentlessly. David and his men came upon Saul as he slept. David, instead of killing Saul, cut off a small corner of his robe as a gesture of respect for God's anointed. Despite his circumstances and discomfort, David allowed the Lord charge over this matter.

JULY 20

*"Their Redeemer is strong,
the LORD of hosts is His name;
He will vigorously plead their case
so that He may bring rest to the earth."*
Jeremiah 50:34

Israel looked forward in time to redemption by the Messiah, while we take a view back in time to the cross on which our Redeemer died. Christ then becomes the central focus for both the Old and New Testaments.

JULY 21

Pilate then took Jesus,
and scourged Him. And the soldiers twisted together
a crown of thorns and put it on His head,
and put on Him a purple robe;
and they began to come up to Him and say,
"Hail, King of the Jews!"
and to give Him slaps in the face.
John 19:1–3

Lord, in my behalf You withstood extreme torture. Am I adding new but invisible wounds each time I refuse to crown You King of my own life?

JULY 22

Now the Philistines were fighting against Israel,
and the men of Israel fled from before the Philistines
and fell slain on Mount Gilboa. The Philistines
overtook Saul and his sons;
and the Philistines killed Jonathan and Abinadab
and Malchi-shua the sons of Saul.
1 Samuel 31:1–2

Who has faithfully stood beside you through life's triumphs and tragedies? For David this person was Jonathan. Father, help me to be a faithful, loving, and unforgettable friend.

JULY 23

"The LORD is in His holy temple.
Let all the earth be silent before Him."
Habakkuk 2:20

*L*ord, instill in my heart a reverence for Your house. May I worship You in spirit and in truth.

JULY 24

Now on the first day of the week
Mary Magdalene came early to the tomb,
while it was still dark, and saw
the stone already taken away from the tomb.
So she ran and came to Simon Peter,
and to the other disciple whom Jesus loved.
John 20:1–2

*P*eter and John ran to the tomb and then left again—too soon, missing the miracle. "But Mary was standing outside the tomb weeping. . . . She turned around, and saw Jesus standing there" (John 20:11, 14).

JULY 25

"The people have fled from the battle,
and also many of the people have fallen and are dead;
and Saul and Jonathan his son are dead also."
2 Samuel 1:4

*D*avid refused to gloat over Saul's death. He poured forth his personal anguish by writing a song for Saul and Jonathan (2 Samuel 1). David turned to God for guidance, and God gave him a fresh call to leadership.

JULY 26

The word of the LORD came expressly
to Ezekiel the priest. . .
in the land of the Chaldeans. . .
and there the hand
of the LORD came upon him.
Ezekiel 1:3

*E*zekiel had been groomed for the priesthood, but that was forever altered when he was taken captive. In captivity, the Lord called him to prophesy concerning Israel's coming restoration and the temple. Lord, despite my own problems and challenges, I can keep going forward as long as You show me a vision of hope.

JULY 27

And when He had spoken this,
He said to him, "Follow Me!" Peter,
turning around, saw the disciple
whom Jesus loved following them. . . .
So Peter seeing him said to Jesus,
"Lord, and what about this man?"
Jesus said to him, "If I want him to
remain until I come, what is that to you?
You follow Me!"
John 21:19–22

Lord, in this special encounter You call me to be accountable for my own walk with you. Please enable me!

JULY 28

And David brought up his men
who were with him, each with his household. . . .
Then the men of Judah came and there anointed
David king over the house of Judah.
2 Samuel 2:3–4

Lord, I know that You appointed David as king of Israel, uniting Your chosen people who were then divided. May I submit my own life to You that You might use me to create unity among believers.

JULY 29

*Then He said to me, "Son of man,
go to the house of Israel and speak
with My words to them."*
Ezekiel 3:4

*H*ow did you become a Christian? By hearing the Word
of God? That's the way I came to know Him as Savior. At
times we are unwilling to risk presenting the gospel message because of personal rejection. However, the outcome
isn't our problem, it's God's. Lord, help me depend on Your
Word to accomplish all You intend.

JULY 30

*"John baptized with water,
but you will be baptized
with the Holy Spirit not many
days from now."*
Acts 1:5

*T*he disciples had learned how to live out the Christian
life from observing Jesus Christ during His three years of
ministry. Now they would watch Christ ascend to heaven;
no longer would they speak to Him face-to-face. However,
Jesus sent them His Spirit, that they might have God's
power within them as His Church began.

July 31

The king said to Nathan the prophet,
". . . The ark of God dwells within tent curtains."
Nathan said to the king,
"Go, do all that is in your mind,
for the LORD is with you."
2 Samuel 7:2–3

*N*athan the prophet supplied David with a quick agreement to his plan to build the temple. However, when Nathan inquired of the Lord, he learned that God had chosen David's son to build the temple. Lord, help me discern Your will.

August 1

Then the Spirit lifted me up,
and I heard a great rumbling sound behind me,
"Blessed be the glory of the LORD in His place."
Ezekiel 3:12

*E*zekiel's vision can be compared to one that John, the writer of the Gospel of John and the Book of Revelation, described. Lord, I'm so grateful that You have intricately woven Your Word for me. Thank You that Your very Spirit enables me to understand these difficult passages.

AUGUST 2

When the day of Pentecost
had come, they were all together in one place.
And suddenly there came from
heaven a noise like a violent
rushing wind, and it filled the whole house
where they were sitting. . . .
And they were all filled with the
Holy Spirit and began to speak with other tongues,
as the Spirit was giving them utterance.
Acts 2:1–2, 4

I honor Your Holy Spirit, not only for insight into Your Word, but for the power to obey You.

AUGUST 3

So David sent and inquired about the woman.
And one said, "Is this not Bathsheba, the daughter
of Eliam, the wife of Uriah the Hittite?"
David sent messengers and took her,
and when she came to him, he lay with her. . . .
The woman conceived.
2 Samuel 11:3–5

*D*avid knew Bathsheba was Uriah's wife but he seduced her anyway. An even greater sin occurred as David tried to cover his tracks. Lord, help me to be accountable to You.

AUGUST 4

"So as I live," declares the Lord GOD, "surely,
because you have defiled My sanctuary
with all your detestable idols and with
all your abominations, therefore I will also withdraw,
and My eye shall have no pity and I will not spare."
Ezekiel 5:11

*G*od always preserves a remnant of His people. And it will be so until the end of time on this earth.

AUGUST 5

"Having been exalted to the right hand of God,
and having received. . .the promise of the Holy Spirit,
He has poured forth this which you both see and hear.
. . . Therefore let all the house of Israel know
for certain that God has made Him
both Lord and Christ—
this Jesus whom you crucified."
Acts 2:33, 36

A fresh new boldness filled the disciples. Jesus Christ had become the bridge between the Old and New Testaments. Everything in history had pointed to this moment. Lord, strengthen my faith.

AUGUST 6

"Because by this deed you have given occasion
to the enemies of the LORD to blaspheme,
the child also that is born
to you shall surely die."
2 Samuel 12:14

*T*he stillborn death of our first child was a devastating blow to my husband and me. As I read this passage of David's suffering, my heart could readily identify with the pain he endured. Gracious Lord, help me look to You for my own help.

AUGUST 7

"So My hand will be against the prophets
who see false visions. . . .
It is definitely because they have
misled My people by saying,
'Peace!' when there is no peace."
Ezekiel 13:9–10

*P*eople today get sick of hearing doomsday forecasters. Those living in Ezekiel's day reacted the same way. They preferred a message of peace rather than hearing of the need for repentance. Lord, help me to share Your truth even in the midst of an apathetic and, yes, hostile world.

AUGUST 8

Then Peter, filled with the Holy Spirit,
said to them, ". . .By the name of Jesus Christ. . .
whom you crucified, whom God raised from the dead—
by this name this man stands here
before you in good health. . . .
And there is salvation in no one else;
for there is no other name under heaven
that has been given among men,
by which we must be saved."
Acts 4:8, 10, 12

What a dynamic change in Peter! To know Christ as Savior is too great a joy to be contained!

AUGUST 9

"The LORD is my rock and my fortress
and my deliverer; My God, my rock,
in whom I take refuge;
My shield and the horn of my salvation,
my stronghold and my refuge; My savior."
2 Samuel 22:2–3

David's understanding of his Lord, using this concept of refuge, is a picture of the peace, comfort, and security we seek for our lives. I praise You only, Jesus, my Rock of Faith and Redeemer.

AUGUST 10

The king talked with them,
and out of them all not one was found like Daniel,
Hananiah, Mishael and Azariah;
so they entered the king's personal service.
And as for every matter of wisdom
and understanding about
which the king consulted them,
he found them ten times better
than all the magicians and conjurers
who were in all his realm.
Daniel 1:19–20

Lord, help me to walk with You that Your will might be accomplished on earth.

AUGUST 11

Peter said to them,
"Repent, and each of you be baptized
in the name of Jesus Christ for the forgiveness
of your sins; and you will receive
the gift of the Holy Spirit."
Acts 2:38

Lord, I thank You that those who lived before Jesus came to earth were given the same gospel message through the prophets. I thank You that You have always provided a way to salvation.

AUGUST 12

As David's time to die drew near,
he charged Solomon his son, saying,
". . .Keep the charge of the LORD your God,
to walk in His ways, to keep His statutes,
His commandments, His ordinances,
and His testimonies, according
to what is written in the Law of Moses."
1 Kings 2:1, 3

One of David's sons, Adonijah, wanted the throne. He planned a full challenge to Solomon's leadership, and it cost him his life. Lord, please help me to graciously accept Your will and be satisfied.

AUGUST 13

Then Nebuchadnezzar. . .said,
"Look! I see four men loosed and
walking about in the midst of the fire
without harm, and the appearance
of the fourth is like a son of the gods!"
Daniel 3:24–25

Jesus was with Daniel's friends in the fire. Lord, be my faithful God, just as You were to Daniel's friends. Keep me from harm as I walk through the fires in my own life.

AUGUST 14

The priests and the captain of the temple guard
and the Sadducees came up to them,
being greatly disturbed because
they were teaching the people and proclaiming
in Jesus the resurrection from the dead.
And they laid hands on them
and put them in jail.
Acts 4:1–3

*B*oth Jesus and John the Baptist had been killed for preaching the truth. Even as Peter and John now spoke, they were arrested. Was their message wasted? Not at all. There will always be a remnant who hears and responds.

AUGUST 15

"So give Your servant an
understanding heart to judge
Your people to discern between good and evil.
For who is able to judge
this great people of Yours?"
1 Kings 3:9

*L*ord, how I pray that such wisdom would be given to lawmakers. I also need Your guidance for my family. Help me remember to turn to You in my dilemmas.

AUGUST 16

When he had come near the den to Daniel,
he cried out with a troubled voice. The king spoke
and said to Daniel, "Daniel, servant of the living God,
has your God, whom you constantly serve,
been able to deliver you from the lions?"
Then Daniel spoke to the king, "O king, live forever!
My God sent His angel and shut the lions' mouths."
Daniel 6:20–22

Lord, I praise You that the next morning, the king found evidence of Your abiding love.

AUGUST 17

Saul was in hearty agreement
with putting him to death. And on that day a great
persecution began against the church in Jerusalem;
and they were all scattered throughout
the regions of Judea and Samaria,
except the apostles.
Acts 8:1

Thank You, God, for changing Saul into Paul!

AUGUST 18

Elisha said, "Please, let a double portion
of your spirit be upon me." He said,
"You have asked a hard thing. Nevertheless,
if you see me when I am taken from you,
it shall be so for you...." As they
were going along and talking, behold,
there appeared a chariot of fire and horses of fire which
separated the two of them. And Elijah went up by a
whirlwind to heaven. Elisha saw it.
2 Kings 2:9–12

Elisha had received God's Spirit. I love God's flair for the dramatic!

AUGUST 19

"Behold, a fourth beast, dreadful and terrifying
and extremely strong; and it had large iron teeth.
It devoured and crushed and trampled down
the remainder with its feet;
and it was different from all the
beasts that were before it."
Daniel 7:7

God made Daniel the recipient of but some of the pieces of this prophetic puzzle. Lord, I know from Your Word that this last terrible beast will be the antichrist. Do not let me be deceived by him.

AUGUST 20

*Now about that time Herod the king
laid hands on some who belonged to the church
in order to mistreat them. And he had James
the brother of John put to death with a sword.*
Acts 12:1–2

*H*is heart filled with grief for a martyred brother, John
must have contemplated his promise of commitment and
then gone on with his ministry. Lord, I know that although
James paid the ultimate price, he now worships before Your
heavenly throne. Help me serve You as well.

AUGUST 21

*They forsook all the commandments
of the LORD their God and made for themselves
molten images. . . . Then they. . .sold themselves
to do evil in the sight of the LORD, provoking Him.
So the LORD was very angry with Israel,
and removed them from His sight.*
2 Kings 17:16–18

*L*ord, what things keep me from Your presence?
Please bring me back into true worship that I might not
be led astray.

AUGUST 22

"From the issuing of a decree to restore
and rebuild Jerusalem until Messiah the Prince
there will be seven weeks and sixty-two weeks;
it will be built again, with plaza and moat,
even in times of distress. Then after
the sixty-two weeks the Messiah will be cut off and have
nothing, and the people of the prince who is to come will
destroy the city and the sanctuary."
Daniel 9:25–26

Jesus, I await Your second coming and the eventual demise of the evil one.

AUGUST 23

And he found a Jew named Aquila. . .
with his wife Priscilla. . . . He came to them,
and because he was of the same trade,
he stayed with them and they were working;
for by trade they were tent-makers.
Acts 18:2–3

Paul worked as a tentmaker so that he might support his travels within his ministry. Lord, show me today how I might serve You and present the gospel message to others.

AUGUST 24

Then David said to Ornan, "Give me
the site of this threshing floor,
that I may build on it an altar to the LORD;
for the full price you shall give it to me,
that the plague may be restrained from the people."
1 Chronicles 21:22

*D*irectly following an incident of King David's disobedience to the Lord which brought a siege of pestilence on the land, God commanded David to obtain a property for the temple. Lord, let me not test Your patience!

AUGUST 25

Then he said to me, "Do not be afraid, Daniel,
for from the first day that you set your heart
on understanding this and on humbling yourself
before your God, your words were heard,
and I have come in response to your words. . . .
Now I have come to give you an understanding
of what will happen to your people in the latter days,
for the vision pertains to the days yet future."
Daniel 10:12, 14

*L*ord, let Your angels protect and enlighten me to truth.

AUGUST 26

Paul, a bond-servant of Christ Jesus, called as an apostle,
set apart for the gospel of God. . .concerning His Son,
who was born of a descendant of David according
to the flesh, who was declared the Son of God
with power by the resurrection from the dead. . .
through whom we have received
grace and apostleship.
Romans 1:1–5

*P*aul had come to know the true source of life. And with this knowledge came a mission for the rest of his days on earth.

AUGUST 27

Solomon amassed chariots and horsemen.
He had 1,400 chariots, and 12,000 horsemen,
and he stationed them in the chariot cities
and with the king at Jerusalem.
2 Chronicles 1:14

*L*ong before Israel even had a king, the Lord had established certain standards for this monarch. He was not to multiply horses for himself, nor cause the people to return to Egypt to get horses (Deuteronomy 17:14–16). God didn't want the king's heart to turn away from following Him.

AUGUST 28

"In his place a despicable person will arise,
on whom the honor of kingship has not been conferred,
but he will come in a time of tranquility
and seize the kingdom by intrigue."
Daniel 11:21

The antichrist is a real person who will one day deviously slither onto the scene. He will appear indispensable at a time of worldwide, unsolvable chaos. Lord, compel me with a new urgency to study Your powerful Word, that I might bring it to others.

AUGUST 29

Do you suppose. . .when you pass judgment
on those who practice such things
and do the same yourself,
that you will escape the judgment of God?
Romans 2:3

Those who know little about the Word of God seem to parade about this verse. Paul was addressing hypocrites who "know the ordinance of God," yet practice things which are "worthy of death" (Romans 1:32). But people recite this verse to those who have the audacity to suggest they should obey God's Word. They try to silence the truth.

AUGUST 30

*Hezekiah became king when he was twenty-five years
old. . . . He did right in the sight of the LORD,
according to all that his father David had done.
In the first year of his reign, in the first month, he opened
the doors of the house of the LORD and repaired them.*
2 Chronicles 29:1–3

Lord, help me learn to abide in You completely.

AUGUST 31

*"Now at that time Michael,
the great prince who stands guard
over the sons of your people, will arise.
And there will be a time of distress
such as never occurred since there was
a nation until that time;
and at that time your people,
everyone who is found written in the book,
will be rescued."*
Daniel 12:1

Lamb of God, who takes away sin, I want to know my
name is written in Your book!

SEPTEMBER 1

For if Abraham was justified by works,
he has something to boast about; but not before God.
For what does the Scripture say?
"ABRAHAM BELIEVED GOD,
AND IT WAS CREDITED TO HIM AS RIGHTEOUSNESS."
Romans 4:2–3

I thank You that I worship a God whose Word can be trusted. I know Jesus will always be there for me.

SEPTEMBER 2

Now in the first year of Cyrus king of Persia,
in order to fulfill the word of the LORD by the mouth
of Jeremiah, the LORD stirred up
the spirit of Cyrus king of Persia,
so that he sent a proclamation
throughout all his kingdom.
Ezra 1:1

*A*pproximately 175 years before King Cyrus was even born, God had spoken through the prophet Isaiah concerning him (Isaiah 44:28). Lord, I am absolutely sure that what You have said will come to pass.

SEPTEMBER 3

When the LORD first spoke through Hosea,
the LORD said to Hosea, "Go, take to yourself
a wife of harlotry
and have children of harlotry;
for the land commits flagrant harlotry,
forsaking the LORD."
Hosea 1:2

*T*he Book of Hosea reveals the brokenness of God's own heart as He watched Israel wander away. "And I will say to those who were not My people, 'You are My people!'" (Hosea 2:23). Lord, thank You for Your unique invitation.

SEPTEMBER 4

Therefore, having been justified by faith,
we have peace with God through our Lord Jesus
Christ, through whom also we have obtained
our introduction by faith into this grace
in which we stand; and we exult
in hope of the glory of God.
Romans 5:1–2

*P*eople have scoured every nook and cranny of the globe in search of peace. But every new road eventually leads to the dead end of dissatisfaction. The only true and lasting peace comes from Jesus Christ.

SEPTEMBER 5

Now when the enemies of Judah and Benjamin
heard that the people of the exile were building
a temple to the LORD God of Israel. . .
then the people of the land discouraged
the people of Judah, and frightened them from building.
Ezra 4:1, 4

*L*ord, You always cause the wicked to stumble. Thank
You!

SEPTEMBER 6

Return to the LORD. Say to Him,
"Take away all iniquity, and receive us graciously,
that we may present the fruit of our lips. . . ."
I will heal their apostasy, I will love them freely,
For My anger has turned away from them.
Hosea 14:2, 4

*O*ur holy God is not obligated to forgive us. Yet what
hope would we have for change if God didn't wipe the slate
of our past failures clean and provide us with the strength
to start afresh?

SEPTEMBER 7

Therefore there is now no condemnation
for those who are in Christ Jesus.
For the law of the Spirit of life in
Christ Jesus has set you free from
the law of sin and of death.
Romans 8:1–2

I rejoice that I am a child of God and heir to the kingdom! Hallelujah!

SEPTEMBER 8

"So, now issue a decree
to make these men stop work,
that this city may not be rebuilt
until a decree is issued by me."
Ezra 4:21

I read that shortly after King Darius issued his decree, work began again to finish the temple. Lord, Your will is always done!

SEPTEMBER 9

What the gnawing locust has left,
the swarming locust has eaten;
And what the swarming locust has left,
the creeping locust has eaten;
And what the creeping locust has left,
the stripping locust has eaten.
Joel 1:4

The information contained in the book of Joel is referred to as eschatology, or a study of the end times, and parallels other passages in scripture. When Jesus spoke to His disciples He, too, quoted this prophetic passage. Lord, I rejoice in Your Word.

SEPTEMBER 10

Brethren, my heart's desire
and my prayer to God for them
is for their salvation.
Romans 10:1

Is the deepest concern of your heart that those whom you love will share heaven with Christ? Lord, clarify Your Word, that we may yield in faith.

SEPTEMBER 11

They said to me, "The remnant there
in the province who survived the
captivity are in great distress and reproach,
and the wall of Jerusalem is broken down
and its gates are burned with fire."
When I heard these words,
I sat down and wept and mourned for days;
and I was fasting and praying
before the God of heaven.
Nehemiah 1:3–4

Lord, let me learn from Nehemiah's example. Let me seek Your will through prayer and study, never losing sight of Your Son.

SEPTEMBER 12

Hasten and come, all you surrounding nations,
And gather yourselves there.
Bring down, O LORD, Your mighty ones.
Joel 3:11

Jerusalem will be the site of the world's last and greatest battle as the surrounding nations rage against the Holy City. The almighty God of the universe will intervene on Israel's behalf. Lord, I don't like to consider the brutality of this final judgment. However, I know that You are fair and just and have given men and women ample time and warning to repent.

SEPTEMBER 13

*I urge you therefore. . .to present your bodies a living
and holy sacrifice, acceptable to God,
which is your spiritual service of worship.
And do not be conformed to this world,
but be transformed by the renewing of your mind.*
Romans 12:1–2

*T*he weapons God provides for us are spiritual. We must become proficient with such an arsenal before it can be effective. So, if the Lord says His Word is a weapon, we've got to read it, know it, and follow it.

SEPTEMBER 14

*And all the people gathered as one man at the square. . .
and they asked Ezra the scribe to bring the
book of the law of Moses. . . .
Then Ezra the priest brought the law
before the assembly of men, women,
and all who could listen with understanding.*
Nehemiah 8:1–2

*T*hrough inspired teamwork, Nehemiah and the remnant of Israel finished rebuilding the wall in only fifty-two days. Nehemiah led the people and relied on God's strength. Lord, let Nehemiah be an example for me.

SEPTEMBER 15

Thus says the LORD, "For three transgressions
of Damascus and for four I will not revoke its
punishment. . . . I will also. . .cut off the inhabitant
from the valley of Aven. . . .
So the people of Aram will go exiled to Kir."
Amos 1:3, 5

*T*hroughout the Old Testament we've read accounts of God's wrath directed toward those whom He loved who were flagrantly disobedient. But God also extended His loving hand of protection to those who walked in obedience.

SEPTEMBER 16

I commend to you our sister Phoebe. . .
that you receive her in the Lord in a manner worthy
of the saints, and that you help her in whatever
matter she may have need of you; for she herself
has also been a helper of many,
and of myself as well.
Romans 16:1–2

*P*aul viewed dedicated people as living testimonies to all that God's Spirit could accomplish in one's character. Lord, as a woman, let my life, as Phoebe's, shine before others.

SEPTEMBER 17

On the seventh day, when the heart of the king
was merry with wine, he commanded...
the seven eunuchs who served in the presence of
King Ahasuerus, to bring Queen Vashti
before the king with her royal crown
in order to display her beauty. . . .
But Queen Vashti refused to come
at the king's command.
Esther 1:10–12

Thank You, Lord God, King of all kings, that You forgive me when I fail to come into Your presence.

SEPTEMBER 18

"Then the house of Jacob will be a fire
And the house of Joseph a flame;
But the house of Esau will be as stubble.
And they will set them on fire and consume them,
So that there will be no survivor of the house of Esau,"
For the LORD has spoken.
Obadiah 1:18

Lord, let me remember that it is Christ who is the
head of His Church and I am but a member of the Body.

SEPTEMBER 19

To those who have been sanctified in Christ Jesus,
saints by calling, with all who in every
place call on the name of our Lord Jesus
Christ, their Lord and ours.
1 Corinthians 1:2

*T*hese Corinthians, whom Paul addressed as saints, were far from model citizens, but he wasn't ashamed to call them brothers. Lord, am I truly Your disciple?

SEPTEMBER 20

Then the king's attendants, who served him, said,
"Let beautiful young virgins be sought for the
king. . . . Then let the young lady who pleases
the king be queen in place of Vashti."
And the matter pleased the king,
and he did accordingly.
Esther 2:2–4

*I*n the beginning, Esther was unaware of how God would use her life. Lord, let me be as available and obedient to You.

SEPTEMBER 21

*"Arise, go to Nineveh the great city
and cry against it, for their wickedness has come
up before Me." But Jonah rose up to flee
to Tarshish from the presence of the LORD.*
Jonah 1:2–3

God had solicited Jonah's help in bringing a message to Ninevah. However, Jonah's fear of these Ninevites loomed far greater than his fear of the Lord. Finally Jonah responded in faith. Lord, please help me yield in the areas You're ready to work on in my life.

SEPTEMBER 22

*For to us God revealed them through the Spirit;
for the Spirit searches all things, even the depths of God
. . . Now we have received. . .the Spirit who is from God,
so that we may know the things freely given to us by God.*
1 Corinthians 2:10, 12

Here's an excuse heard often: "We can't try to interpret the Bible ourselves because we'll get confused." But to refuse the Holy Spirit the opportunity to instruct you, as He promised He would, is to refuse true understanding.

SEPTEMBER 23

In those days, while Mordecai was sitting
at the king's gate, Bigthan and Teresh,
two of the king's officials from those who guarded the door,
became angry and sought to lay hands on King Ahasuerus.
But the plot became known to Mordecai
and he told Queen Esther,
and Esther informed the king in Mordecai's name.
Esther 2:21–22

Lord, what a dark hour this was for Your people, but You had already put a plan into action.

SEPTEMBER 24

So they picked up Jonah, threw him into the sea,
and the sea stopped its raging. . . .
And the LORD appointed a great fish to swallow Jonah,
and Jonah was in the stomach
of the fish three days and three nights.
Jonah 1:15, 17

Lord, You alone have the ability to deliver a great fish to swallow a man whole and not harm him. Help me trust You for creative solutions to all my problems.

SEPTEMBER 25

*Do you not know that you are a temple of God
and that the Spirit of God dwells in you?
If any man destroys the temple of God,
God will destroy him, for the temple of God is holy,
and that is what you are.*
1 Corinthians 3:16–17

Lord, let me live as though I believe You are permeating my very being. Amen.

SEPTEMBER 26

*Then the king's scribes were summoned
on the thirteenth day of the first month,
and it was written just as Haman
commanded to the king's satraps. . . .
And letters were sent by couriers to
all the king's provinces to destroy,
to kill, and to annihilate all the Jews.*
Esther 3:12–13

Mordecai replied, "Who knows whether you have not attained royalty for such a time as this?" (Esther 4:14). Esther trusted God. I praise Him!

SEPTEMBER 27

"I called out of my distress to the LORD,
and He answered me. I cried for help from the
depth of Sheol; You heard my voice."...
Then the LORD commanded the fish,
and it vomited Jonah up onto the dry land.
Jonah 2:2, 10

*N*ow the Lord issued to Jonah a fresh call to go to Ninevah, that he might get the response right this time.

SEPTEMBER 28

Does any one of you, when he has a case
against his neighbor, dare to go to law before
the unrighteous and not before the saints? ...
Do you not know that we will judge angels?
How much more matters of this life?
1 Corinthians 6:1, 3

*T*he verses above are meant to give you hope. The saints of God will one day judge those who operate within this world system of injustice. As God brings down justice, this world will be held accountable to Him.

SEPTEMBER 29

So Esther replied,
"My petition and my request is:
if I have found favor in the sight of the king,
and if it pleases the king to grant my petition
and do what I request, may the king
and Haman come to the banquet which
I will prepare for them, and tomorrow
I will do as the king says."
Esther 5:7–8

Lord, thank You for giving Esther the wisdom and courage to save her people and Your people, the Jews.

SEPTEMBER 30

When God saw their deeds, that they turned
from their wicked way, then God relented
concerning the calamity which He had declared
He would bring upon them.
And He did not do it.
Jonah 3:10

I praise my compassionate God!

OCTOBER 1

It is good for a man not to touch a woman.
But because of immoralities, each man is to
have his own wife, and each woman is to have her own
husband. . . . But this I say by way of concession,
not of command.
1 Corinthians 7:1–2, 6

If a woman can best serve God as part of a married couple, then the Lord will provide the mate she seeks. Single or married, show me how to make a difference, Lord.

OCTOBER 2

Then Esther spoke again to the king,
fell at his feet, wept, and implored him to avert
the evil scheme of Haman the Agagite and his
plot which he had devised against the Jews.
The king extended the golden scepter to Esther.
Esther 8:3–4

Lord, I thank You for this account of Esther's obedience, loyalty, and trust.

OCTOBER 3

Hear, O peoples, all of you; Listen,
O earth and all it contains,
And let the Lord GOD be a witness against you,
The Lord from His holy temple.
For behold, the LORD is coming forth from His place.
He will come down and tread
on the high places of the earth.
Micah 1:2–3

*L*ord, keep me from following in the footsteps of the rebellious, that I might not require bitter lessons of truth.

OCTOBER 4

Who at any time serves as a soldier
at his own expense? Who plants a vineyard,
and does not eat the fruit of it?
Or who tends a flock and does
not use the milk of the flock?
1 Corinthians 9:7

*P*aul choose to labor without receiving any wages so that no one could accuse him of presenting the gospel for personal gain. Lord, let me remember in my prayers, tithes, and offerings all those who labor to bring the Word of God to me and others.

OCTOBER 5

There was a man. . .whose name was Job;
and that man was blameless, upright,
fearing God and turning away from evil.
Seven sons and three daughters
were born to him. His possessions also were 7,000 sheep,
3,000 camels, 500 yoke of oxen,
500 female donkeys.
Job 1:1–3

This, of course, was life as Job used to know it, before his character was tested. His life became an unwelcome ride on a trolley called tragedy. And through all of this, Job refused to blame God or to sin.

OCTOBER 6

Woe to those who scheme iniquity,
Who work out evil on their beds!
When morning comes, they do it,
For it is in the power of their hands.
Micah 2:1

Lord, guard my mind from evil that I might not ruminate on such things and be propelled into ungodly actions. Instead, let me turn to Your Word which acts as a cleansing agent.

OCTOBER 7

Now these things happened as examples for us,
so that we would not crave evil things, as they also craved.
. . . Nor let us act immorally, as some of them did,
and twenty-three thousand fell in one day.
1 Corinthians 10:6, 8

*B*y reading the entire Bible we have the privilege of learning from God's dealings with men and women throughout recorded history so we will not fall into the same traps. Father, help me avoid temptation by taking one step closer to You.

OCTOBER 8

"Oh that my grief were actually weighed,
and laid in the balances together with my calamity!
For then it would be heavier than the sand of the seas. . . .
But it is still my consolation,
and I rejoice in unsparing pain,
that I have not denied the words
of the Holy One."
Job 6:2–3, 10

*D*o we stand on the bedrock of knowledge about God's goodness, despite the circumstances? Or do we succumb to the opinions of friends?

OCTOBER 9

And He will arise and shepherd His flock
In the strength of the LORD, in the majesty
of the name of the LORD His God.
And they will remain, Because at that time
He will be great to the ends of the earth.
This One will be our peace.
Micah 5:4–5

I rejoice because Christ is coming back! "On His robe and on His thigh He has a name written, 'KING OF KINGS, AND LORD OF LORDS'" (Revelation 19:16).

OCTOBER 10

Therefore I make known to you
that no one speaking by the Spirit of God says,
"Jesus is accursed"; and no one can say,
"Jesus is Lord," except by the Holy Spirit.
1 Corinthians 12:3

*L*ord, I know if I'm listening to a message that makes me depressed and defeated, that's from Satan. I know the message that says I'm worth dying for is from Christ.

OCTOBER 11

"It is God who removes the mountains. . .
Who alone stretches out the heavens,
And tramples down the waves of the sea;
Who makes the Bear, Orion, and the Pleiades. . .
Who does great things, unfathomable,
And wondrous works without number."
Job 9:5, 8–10

The God who has created all that we see, hear, touch, taste, and smell is able to control what we don't understand. Job recognized that both blessings and testing through trials flowed from the same loving hands.

OCTOBER 12

What does the LORD require of you
But to do justice, to love kindness,
And to walk humbly with your God?
Micah 6:8

Christ has already paid the price that needed to be exacted for our sins. The God of this universe became a man, and then He sacrificed His life so that we who could never deserve His mercy might obtain it. Jesus did all this because He is both just and kind.

OCTOBER 13

If I speak with the tongues of men and of angels,
but do not have love, I have become
a noisy gong or a clanging cymbal.
1 Corinthians 13:1

*E*ven though we've prayed for godly mates, and then relied on God's guidance, there will still be times when our
attempts to love are less than perfect. However, if both man
and woman turn back to God's blueprint, harmony can be
restored.

OCTOBER 14

"Speak to the earth, and let it teach you;
And let the fish of the sea declare to you.
Who among all these does not know
That the hand of the LORD has done this,
In whose hand is the life of every living thing,
And the breath of all mankind?"
Job 12:8–10

*L*ord, I know that even if I didn't have Your written
Word, the order and perfection of Your creation still prove
Your existence!

OCTOBER 15

And the earth will become desolate because
of her inhabitants, on account of the fruit
of their deeds. Shepherd Your people with Your scepter,
the flock of Your possession which dwells by itself
in the woodland, in the midst of a fruitful field.
Let them feed in Bashan and Gilead
as in the days of old.
Micah 7:13–14

I look forward to meeting my Shepherd!

OCTOBER 16

But now Christ has been raised from the dead,
the first fruits of those who are asleep.
For since by a man came death, by a man also came
the resurrection of the dead. For as in Adam all die,
so also in Christ all will be made alive.
1 Corinthians 15:20–22

F rom man's beginning in the Garden of Eden, one Savior was promised (Genesis 3:15).

OCTOBER 17

And the LORD restored the fortunes of Job. . . .
And the LORD blessed the latter days of Job more than
his beginning, and he had 14,000 sheep, and 6,000 camels,
and 1,000 yoke of oxen, and 1,000 female donkeys.
He had seven sons and three daughters.
Job 42:10, 12–13

*L*ord, through Job's pain, agony, and loss, You placed "wisdom in his innermost being" concerning deep and marvelous truths about Your character. When I am afflicted, remind me to turn toward You.

OCTOBER 18

Behold, on the mountains the feet of him
who brings good news, who announces peace!
Celebrate your feasts, O Judah. . .
For never again will the wicked one pass through you;
He is cut off completely.
Nahum 1:15

*N*o news could be sweeter than the prophecy that a mighty enemy army was about to suffer a great demise. God gave Nahum just such a vision. Nahum then extolled the virtues of His God so that when God acted, the enemy would know exactly whom they had encountered.

OCTOBER 19

Blessed be the God and Father of our Lord Jesus Christ,
the Father of mercies and God of all comfort;
who comforts us in all our affliction so that we will
be able to comfort those who are in any affliction
with the comfort with which we ourselves
are comforted by God.
2 Corinthians 1:3–4

*T*his is the purpose of our trials, that we might comfort one another and lean on the Lord's strength.

OCTOBER 20

If then you regard me a partner, accept him
as you would me. But if he has wronged
you in any way, or owes you anything,
charge that to my account.
Philemon 1:17–18

*F*ather, thank You that my sins have been charged to Christ's account. Thank You that He paid the debt.

OCTOBER 21

But the righteous will live by his faith.
Habakkuk 2:4

*I*n whom is our faith placed? If our faith is in Christ, we are established upon firm ground. But if it's in systems, programs, or even religion, it's doomed to fail.

OCTOBER 22

I know a man in Christ who fourteen years ago. . .
was caught up into Paradise, and heard inexpressible
words, which a man is not permitted to speak.
On behalf of such a man I will boast;
but on my own behalf I will not boast,
except in regard to my weaknesses.
2 Corinthians 12:2, 4–5

*L*ord, Your magnificent presence is all I need to provide me with the momentum to continue spreading Your Word.

OCTOBER 23

God, after He spoke long ago to the fathers in the prophets...
in these last days has spoken to us in His Son. ...
When He had made purification of sins,
He sat down at the right hand
of the Majesty on high.
Hebrews 1:1–3

*T*he book of Hebrews confirmed to those who had left the rituals of Judaism that they still had a high priest who could petition the Father for them. He is Jesus Christ, their Messiah, our Savior and Lord.

OCTOBER 24

"Then it will come about on
the day of the LORD's sacrifice,
that I will punish the princes,
the king's sons and all who clothe
themselves with foreign garments."
Zephaniah 1:8

*Z*ephaniah's call from the Lord involved dislodging those who were indifferent to God. The latest opinion polls show that a majority of us in America claim to believe in God. But how is faith evidenced? As surely as judgment fell upon Israel for their sins, it will ultimately fall on us.

October 25

I am amazed that you are so quickly deserting
Him who called you by the grace of Christ,
for a different gospel. . .there are some
who are disturbing you and want
to distort the gospel of Christ.
Galatians 1:6–7

Jewish believers were transitioning from the law, filled with regulations, and to the gospel of grace. A group began wooing them back to the old legalism. Therefore, Paul left on journeys to bring the gospel of grace to those who were being seduced by this group.

October 26

Therefore, holy brethren, partakers of a heavenly
calling, consider Jesus, the Apostle and High Priest
of our confession; He was faithful to Him
who appointed Him, as Moses also was in all
His house. For He has been counted worthy
of more glory than Moses, by just so
much as the builder of the house has
more honor than the house.
Hebrews 3:1–3

The opportunity to follow Christ lies before me. Lord, help me respond.

OCTOBER 27

Seek the LORD, all you humble of the earth
who have carried out His ordinances;
seek righteousness, seek humility.
Perhaps you will be hidden
in the day of the LORD's anger.
Zephaniah 2:3

*T*hank You, Father, that prayer can place me in Your presence.

OCTOBER 28

For am I now seeking the favor of men, or of God?
Or am I striving to please men?
If I were still trying to please men,
I would not be a bond-servant of Christ.
Galatians 1:10

*P*aul didn't sit around asking men for their opinions. Christ's call was sufficient. Therefore, he devoted himself to study, prayer, and meditation alone with his Lord. What are my own misconceptions concerning Your Word, Lord? Teach me the true meaning of the scriptures.

OCTOBER 29

For it is written that Abraham had two sons,
one by the bondwoman and
one by the free woman.
Galatians 4:22

Paul uses these two sons to illustrate the status of the unbeliever versus her changed relationship once she commits her life to Christ. Once we were slaves to sin, but with our redemption in Christ, we become free.

OCTOBER 30

"Thus says the LORD of hosts, 'This people says,
"The time has not come, even the time for
the house of the LORD to be rebuilt."' "
Then the word of the LORD came by Haggai . . .
saying, "Is it time for you yourselves
to dwell in your paneled houses
while this house lies desolate?"
Now therefore, thus says the LORD of hosts,
"Consider your ways!"
Haggai 1:2–5

Lord, whatever task is overwhelming me today, You have the strength to see it through to fulfillment.

OCTOBER 31

Therefore, let us fear if, while a promise remains of entering
His rest, any. . .may seem to have come short of it.
For indeed we have had good news preached to us,
just as they also; but the word they heard
did not profit them, because it was not
united by faith in those who heard.
Hebrews 4:1–2

*D*ear God, You have kept Your part of the bargain, in obtaining salvation for me. Whether I respond to this salvation is up to me.

NOVEMBER 1

For this Melchizedek, king of Salem, priest
of the Most High God. . .was first of all,
by the translation of his name, king of righteousness,
and then also. . .king of peace. Without father,
without mother, without genealogy,
having neither beginning of days nor end of life,
but made like the Son of God,
he remains a priest perpetually.
Hebrews 7:1–3

*M*elchizedek's priesthood is a perpetual one. The Levitical priesthood, no longer necessary after Christ's death on the cross, ended when the temple was destroyed.

NOVEMBER 2

I saw at night, and behold, a man was riding
on a red horse. . . . Then I said, "My lord, what are these?"
. . . And the man who was standing among
the myrtle trees answered and said,
"These are those whom the LORD
has sent to patrol the earth."
Zechariah 1:8–10

Zechariah's name means "God remembers." The message he received from the Lord came at a time when Israel most needed to be reminded that their God still stood watch over them.

NOVEMBER 3

But the fruit of the Spirit is love, joy,
peace, patience, kindness, goodness, faithfulness,
gentleness, self-control; against
such things there is no law.
Galatians 5:22–23

Why is God showering us with these gifts? Because they prove that He can enter a human life and affect her or him with change, that others might also be won to Christ as they observe this miracle.

NOVEMBER 4

James, a bond-servant of God and
of the Lord Jesus Christ, To the twelve tribes
who are dispersed abroad: Greetings.
Consider it all joy, my brethren,
when you encounter various trials,
knowing that the testing of your
faith produces endurance.
James 1:1–3

How grateful I am, Lord, that You're not willing that any should perish, especially those of Your own family.

NOVEMBER 5

"Jerusalem will be inhabited without walls
because of the multitude of men and cattle within it.
'For I,' declares the LORD,
'will be a wall of fire around her,
and I will be the glory in her midst.'"
Zechariah 2:4–5

At a time when only a remnant of Israel had returned to Jerusalem, the Lord promised that at a future time they would become a great nation. How grateful I am, Lord, to know that Your might and unlimited power protect Israel.

NOVEMBER 6

Blessed be the God and Father of our Lord Jesus Christ,
who has blessed us with every spiritual blessing
in the heavenly places in Christ,
just as He chose us in Him before the
foundation of the world, that we
would be holy and blameless before Him.
Ephesians 1:3–4

Lord, help me and each woman reading this to enjoy the safety, protection, and sense of belonging that come from being chosen by You.

NOVEMBER 7

You see that faith was working with his works,
and as a result of the works, faith was perfected;
and the Scripture was fulfilled which says,
"And Abraham believed God, and it was reckoned
to him as righteousness,"
and he was called the friend of God.
James 2:22–23

Abraham's faith was evident by his actions. No matter what God required of him, Abraham obeyed God. Therefore, all of his actions were born out of the call God had on his life.

NOVEMBER 8

"The LORD will possess Judah as His portion
in the holy land, and will again choose Jerusalem.
Be silent, all flesh, before the LORD;
for He is aroused from His holy habitation."
Zechariah 2:12–13

*T*rue holiness cannot reign within Israel until the Messiah, Jesus Christ, comes to inhabit this nation. Jesus will finally reign as Israel's true King.

NOVEMBER 9

In Him, you also. . .were sealed in Him
with the Holy Spirit of promise,
who is given as a pledge of our inheritance.
Ephesians 1:13–14

*S*ealing waxes and metal impressions were used in the past as both a security measure and a statement of authenticity. The king's signet ring was pressed into hot melted wax, leaving an indelible and unique impression. Paul was inspired to use this image to describe how we, as believers, are sealed by God's Holy Spirit.

NOVEMBER 10

So also the tongue is a small part of the body,
and yet it boasts of great things.
See how great a forest is set aflame
by such a small fire!
And the tongue is a fire.
James 3:5–6

*W*e all have difficulty either saying too much or not saying it right. Thank You, Jesus, for Your Words of infinite wisdom.

NOVEMBER 11

Now Joshua was clothed with filthy garments
and standing before the angel. He spoke
and said to those who were standing before him,
saying, "Remove the filthy garments from him."
Again he said to him, "See, I have taken
your iniquity away from you
and will clothe you with festal robes."
Zechariah 3:3–4

*G*od has provided the means for our atonement and will do all in His power to lead us to the foot of the cross that we might obtain it.

NOVEMBER 12

Wives, be subject to your own husbands,
as to the Lord. For the husband is the head
of the wife, as Christ also is the head
of the church.
Ephesians 5:22–23

*W*ives, our role is that of a helpmate, not a doormat. It's critical to remember that God intended marriage to be a partnership. Only the Lord is capable of loving perfectly. So the next time your marriage feels like a 90/10 proposition, remember that He's giving 100 percent.

NOVEMBER 13

According to the foreknowledge of God the Father,
by the sanctifying work of the Spirit,
to obey Jesus Christ and be sprinkled
with His blood: May grace
and peace be yours in fullest measure.
1 Peter 1:2

*J*esus Christ will never fail us. He alone possesses perfectly all the characteristics we most admire, for He remains faithful, just, loving, omnipotent, and eternal.

November 14

And the angel of the LORD admonished Joshua saying,
"Thus says the LORD of hosts, 'If you will walk in My
ways...then you will also govern My house and also
have charge of My courts, and I will grant
you free access among these who are standing here.'"
Zechariah 3:6–7

*A*s incredible an offer as this might have been for Joshua, an even more miraculous invitation awaits those who accept Jesus as Savior. For immediately they can enjoy the very presence of God.

November 15

I thank my God in all my remembrance of you,
always offering prayer with joy in my every prayer
for you all, in view of your participation
in the gospel from the first day until now.
Philippians 1:3–5

*P*aul was confined to prison when he wrote this letter. His joy was not dependent upon circumstances. Rather, it overflowed from the content of his heart, where the true source of joy resides, Jesus Christ.

NOVEMBER 16

In this you greatly rejoice, even though
now for a little while, if necessary,
you have been distressed by various trials,
so that the proof of your faith, being
more precious than gold which is perishable,
even though tested by fire, may be found
to result in praise and glory
and honor at the revelation of Jesus Christ.
1 Peter 1:6–7

What degree of persecution are you willing to endure that the gospel of truth might go forward to a needy world? Thank You, Jesus, for convicting my soul today.

NOVEMBER 17

"For behold, the stone that I have set before Joshua;
on one stone are seven eyes.
Behold, I will engrave an inscription on it,"
declares the LORD of hosts,
"and I will remove the iniquity
of that land in one day."
Zechariah 3:9

The rock which Zechariah describes here is Jesus Christ, Israel's Messiah. Fulfilling Old Testament prophecy, the Israelites rejected this cornerstone. Lord, help me cherish the truth concerning the Messiah's identity.

NOVEMBER 18

Do nothing from selfishness or empty conceit,
but with humility of mind regard
one another as more important than yourselves;
do not merely look out for your own personal interests,
but also for the interests of others.
Philippians 2:3–4

*A*s Christians we are called to encourage one another in the faith. Paul, who spent so much of his own life in prison, had a deep understanding of the need for the reassurance and hope which the Lord richly supplied.

NOVEMBER 19

Therefore, putting aside all malice and all deceit
and hypocrisy and envy and all slander,
like newborn babes, long for the pure milk of the word,
so that by it you may grow in respect to salvation,
if you have tasted the kindness of the Lord.
1 Peter 2:1–3

*A*s mothers, grandmothers, stepmothers, and aunts, we have a God-ordained call to teach children the Word of God that they might someday enter the kingdom of God.

NOVEMBER 20

*"I see, and behold, a lampstand all of gold with its bowl
on the top of it, and its seven lamps on it
with seven spouts belonging to each
of the lamps which are on the top of it."*
Zechariah 4:2

God's purpose for these visions was to motivate Israel to rebuild the temple. The seven-branched lampstand reminded Zechariah of the candelabra which the Jews call the menorah. The menorah was used in the temple as a natural light within the holy place.

NOVEMBER 21

*Therefore, my beloved brethren whom I long to see,
my joy and crown, in this way stand firm in the Lord,
my beloved. I urge Euodia and I urge Syntyche
to live in harmony in the Lord.*
Philippians 4:1–2

Lord, help me to remember that You surrendered all Your rights that I might know true freedom. Please show me how to persevere, make amends, and live in harmony.

NOVEMBER 22

In the same way, you wives,
be submissive to your own husbands
so that even if any of them are disobedient to the word,
they may be won without a word by
the behavior of their wives,
as they observe your chaste
and respectful behavior.
1 Peter 3:1–2

Lord, show me Your way through my difficulties. If my spouse or boyfriend does not know You as his Savior, help me lead by example.

NOVEMBER 23

Then I said to him,
"What are these two olive trees
on the right of the lampstand and on its left?"...
Then he said, "These are the two anointed ones."
Zechariah 4:11, 14

While they are symbolically referred to as "olive branches," these are two men who spread the gospel to the Jews during the tribulation period. Lord, I pray that those in Israel will listen to the message of Your witnesses, that many might be saved.

November 24

Praying always for you, since we heard
of your faith in Christ Jesus. . .
because of the hope laid up for you in heaven,
of which you previously heard in the word of truth,
the gospel, which has come to you.
Colossians 1:3–6

*T*he culture of these people in Colosse was steeped in Oriental mysticism. They lived along the main trade route, which made for a variety of backgrounds and doctrines. Paul reaches out to this nucleus of believers that their foundation in Christ might remain strong.

November 25

His divine power has granted to us everything
pertaining to life and godliness, through the
true knowledge of Him who called us by
His own glory and excellence.
For by these He has granted to us
His precious and magnificent promises,
so that by them you may
become partakers of the divine nature.
2 Peter 1:3–4

*A*s we walk in step with Him, learning His ways, we will eventually reflect these changes in our character.

NOVEMBER 26

The word of the LORD of hosts came to me, saying,
"Say to all the people of the land and to the priests,
'When you fasted and mourned in the fifth
and seventh months these seventy years,
was it actually for Me that you fasted?'"
Zechariah 7:4–5

God wanted His people to celebrate joyously with a sense of gratitude to Him. Instead, the Israelites had made nothing but rituals out of the holy days. Lord, help me to love You with my whole heart.

NOVEMBER 27

He is the image of the invisible God,
the firstborn of all creation. For by Him all things
were created, both in the heavens and on earth,
visible and invisible, whether thrones or dominions
or rulers or authorities—
all things have been created
through Him and for Him.
Colossians 1:15–16

Jesus Christ lived a sinless life, and died on the cross of Calvary for my sins. I worship the King of kings!

November 28

By the word of God the heavens
existed long ago and the earth was formed
out of water and by water, through which
the world at that time was destroyed,
being flooded with water.
2 Peter 3:5–6

How could a loving God destroy the very people and their world which He created? Look at how much time He provided for them to repent. From the time Noah received the order to build the ark until the rain began, a span of 120 years had elapsed.

November 29

"Behold, I am going to send My messenger,
and he will clear the way before Me.
And the LORD, whom you seek, will suddenly
come to His temple; and the messenger
of the covenant, in whom you delight,
behold, He is coming," says the LORD of hosts.
Malachi 3:1

Jesus Christ, God's promise to the world has come! Thank You for Your Word of Truth.

NOVEMBER 30

When Christ, who is our life, is revealed,
then you also will be revealed with Him in glory.
Therefore consider the members of your earthly body
as dead to immorality, impurity, passion,
evil desire, and greed,
which amounts to idolatry.
Colossians 3:4–5

Our churches are comprised of redeemed sinners. Christ in us should make a visible difference in how we are living our lives. For Christ has set up residence within us.

DECEMBER 1

We have seen and testify and proclaim
to you the eternal life, which was
with the Father and was manifested to us.
1 John 1:2

Where will you find joy this Christmas? It's not in brightly colored packages under the tree. And unless your loved ones know the Lord, jubilation probably won't be present at your family gatherings either. Dear Lord, thank You for the knowledge that Jesus is still the "reason for the season."

DECEMBER 2

The Revelation of Jesus Christ, which God
gave Him to show to His bond-servants,
the things which must soon take place;
and He sent and communicated it by
His angel to His bond-servant John,
who testified to the word of God
and to the testimony of Jesus Christ,
even to all that he saw.
Revelation 1:1–2

After God gave Malachi the prophecies concerning the Messiah's coming, He remained silent for over 400 years. And then He spoke to us. . .through His blessed Son, Jesus Christ.

DECEMBER 3

There is no distinction between Greek and Jew,
circumcised and uncircumcised, barbarian,
Scythian, slave and freeman,
but Christ is all, and in all.
Colossians 3:11

To say we love Christ and yet maintain deeply rooted prejudices against others is inconsistent with everything He taught. Lord, let the true peace of Christmas, which is Christ, be found in my heart as I am obedient to Your command to love others just as You have loved me.

DECEMBER 4

See how great a love the Father
has bestowed on us,
that we would be called children of God;
and such we are. . . .
Beloved, now we are children of God.
1 John 3:1–2

*L*ord, as I prepare to celebrate Your birth, the greatest gift I can lay beside the manger is an act of my will that makes me Your child. Yes, I have been born again.

DECEMBER 5

BEHOLD, HE IS COMING WITH THE CLOUDS,
and every eye will see Him,
even those who pierced Him;
and all the tribes of the earth
will mourn over Him. So it is to be.
Amen.
Revelation 1:7

*F*ather, when humans have failed me I tend to blame You for their choices. Please break down the barriers in my heart that I might worship Your Son this Christmas.

DECEMBER 6

We give thanks to God always for all of you,
making mention of you in our prayers; constantly
bearing in mind your work of faith and labor
of love and steadfastness of hope in our
Lord Jesus Christ in the presence
of our God and Father.
1 Thessalonians 1:2–3

God meant for His church to be dynamic. This is the place where His believers still gather to worship and grow. Lord, help me to spread the gospel to those yet unsaved around me.

DECEMBER 7

The eyes of the LORD are toward the righteous,
And His ears are open to their cry.
Psalm 34:15

The Spirit of God hears our cries and takes our petitions before the Father who answers our prayers, for we have confessed belief in Him.

DECEMBER 8

"But I have this against you,
that you have left your first love."
Revelation 2:4

There is nothing to compare with that "first bloom of love." This is the kind of love which God desires from us—that on-fire, totally consuming, single focus of our attention. O Lord, may Your Light be the fire in my soul!

DECEMBER 9

Therefore encourage one another,
and build up one another. . . .
Appreciate those who diligently labor among you,
and have charge over you in the Lord
and give you instruction. . .
esteem them very highly in love
because of their work. Live in
peace with one another.
1 Thessalonians 5:11–13

God equates love with obedience. When Christ returns for His believers, we are to be found walking in His statutes. Lord, let me be found obediently living Your call and commission.

DECEMBER 10

Whoever believes that Jesus
is the Christ is born of God,
and whoever loves the Father
loves the child born of Him.
1 John 5:1

When our children disobey, we feel not only extreme disappointment but a sense that they don't love us. If they did, they would understand that our instructions are meant to guide them over the rough terrain of life. This is exactly how God feels when we fail to follow Him, for He equates love with obedience.

DECEMBER 11

Behold, a throne was standing in heaven,
and One sitting on the throne.
And He who was sitting was like a jasper stone
and a sardius in appearance;
and there was a rainbow around the throne,
like an emerald in appearance.
Revelation 4:2–3

This rainbow in heaven is not the half-bow we're used to seeing. It is a complete circle because in heaven all things are whole and finished. The most amazing thing about this prism of color is that it surrounds Christ.

DECEMBER 12

We request you, brethren, with regard
to the coming of our Lord Jesus Christ
and our gathering together to Him,
that you not be quickly shaken
from your composure or be disturbed either
by a spirit or a message…
to the effect that the day of the Lord has come.
Let no one in any way deceive you,
for it will not come unless the apostasy comes first,
and the man of lawlessness is revealed.
2 Thessalonians 2:1–3

*E*ven so, come Lord Jesus!

DECEMBER 13

Grace, mercy and peace will be with us,
from God the Father and from Jesus Christ,
the Son of the Father, in truth and love.
2 John 1:3

*J*esus Christ. . .heralded by a star, proclaimed by angels, announced by the shepherds, and given by the Father to a world in need of a Savior. O, come let me adore Him!

DECEMBER 14

I saw in the right hand of Him who
sat on the throne a book. . . .
Then I began to weep greatly,
because no one was found worthy to open the book. . .
and one of the elders said to me,
"Stop weeping; behold, the Lion that
is from the tribe of Judah. . .
has overcome so as to open the book."
Revelation 5:1, 4–5

*L*ord, I can't truly celebrate Christmas unless I know that Jesus is God in the flesh, born to die for my sins.

DECEMBER 15

To Timothy, my true child in the faith:
Grace, mercy and peace from God the Father
and Christ Jesus our Lord. . . .
The goal of our instruction is love
from a pure heart and a good conscience
and a sincere faith.
1 Timothy 1:2, 5

*P*aul wrote this letter to encourage Timothy in his own leadership role, knowing that the worst thing this young believer could do was to try and emulate Paul instead of Christ. Lord, show me how to use my special gifts.

DECEMBER 16

Anyone who. . .does not abide in the teaching of Christ,
does not have God. . . . If anyone comes to you
and does not bring this teaching,
do not receive him into your house.
2 John 1:9–10

*T*here is no greater evil than to fail to recognize who Jesus Christ is, God in the flesh. Today's scripture warns against false teachings. Lord, strengthen my faith so that I can love those who don't know You, so that I can reveal the true identity of Your Son.

DECEMBER 17

And I looked, and behold, a white horse,
and he who sat on it had a bow; and a crown
was given to him; and he went out conquering
and to conquer. And when He broke the second seal,
I heard the second living creature saying, "Come."
And another, a red horse, went out.
Revelation 6:2–4

*E*ach of the four horsemen represents a different judgment that will come upon the earth. Lord, please help me understand Your Word.

DECEMBER 18

First of all, then, I urge that entreaties and prayers,
petitions and thanksgivings,
be made on behalf of all men.
1 Timothy 2:1

*P*rayer is an act of worship on the part of the created toward the Creator. It is simply "talking to God" about everything that affects our lives. Spirit of God, fall afresh on me that I might lift my voice in petition to You.

DECEMBER 19

Beloved, you are acting faithfully in
whatever you accomplish for the brethren,
and especially when they are strangers;
and they have testified to your love
before the church. You will
do well to send them on their way
in a manner worthy of God.
3 John 1:5–6

*F*ather, my church will likely be filled this Christmas with people who may only come once or twice a year. May I give these inquiring minds a warm reception.

December 20

I looked, and behold, an ashen horse;
and he who sat on it had the name Death;
and Hades was following with him.
Authority was given to them over
a fourth of the earth, to kill with sword
and with famine and with pestilence
and by the wild beasts of the earth.
Revelation 6:8

*I*n this vision, first came Death and Hades followed. Although Death claims the body and Hades the soul, only Jesus Christ holds the keys of Death and Hades.

December 21

An overseer, then, must be above reproach,
the husband of one wife, temperate, prudent,
respectable, hospitable, able to teach,
not addicted to wine or pugnacious,
but gentle, peaceable,
free from the love of money.
1 Timothy 3:2–3

*A*lthough this passage may appear directed toward men, it applies to women as well. For the position of deacon, referred to as a servant who assisted the apostles, Paul singled out Phoebe, a deaconess, for special recognition (Romans 16:1–2).

DECEMBER 22

And I saw another angel ascending
from the rising of the sun,
having the seal of the living God;
and he cried out with a loud voice to the four angels. . .
saying, "Do not harm the earth or the sea or the trees
until we have sealed the bond-servants
of our God on their foreheads."
Revelation 7:2–3

Jesus Christ, the Alpha and Omega, is the King of kings and Lord of lords. And He's coming back! Hallelujah!

DECEMBER 23

I thank God. . .as I constantly remember
you in my prayers night and day, longing to see you,
even as I recall your tears, so that I may be filled with joy.
For I am mindful of the sincere
faith within you.
2 Timothy 1:3–5

Paul had to make sure that Timothy remained strong in the faith. For Timothy would now "carry the torch of faith" and continue bringing the gospel to all who would listen. Like Timothy, use me, Lord, to do Your will.

DECEMBER 24

Beloved, while I was making every effort
to write you about our common salvation,
I felt the necessity to write to you appealing
that you contend earnestly for the faith
which was once for all handed down to the saints.
Jude 1:3

*I*t's Christmas Eve, and you probably have a busy day ahead. Has the luster of Christmas worn off, replaced by the worldly pressures that overshadow Christ's birth? Jesus, remind me today to set aside time to be with You.

DECEMBER 25

While they were there,
the days were completed for her to give birth.
And she gave birth to her firstborn son;
and she wrapped Him in cloths,
and laid Him in a manger,
because there was no room
for them in the inn.
Luke 2:6–7

*J*oy fills our hearts as we celebrate Christmas. Thank You, Jesus, for willingly leaving heaven's throne to take on a human body and grow to manhood so You could die on the cross.

DECEMBER 26

Grace and peace from God the Father
and Christ Jesus our Savior. For this reason
I left you in Crete, that you would
set in order what remains.
Titus 1:4–5

Lord, have I lived my life this year in a way that pleased you?

DECEMBER 27

"And I will grant authority
to my two witnesses,
and they will prophesy for
twelve hundred and sixty days,
clothed in sackcloth."
These are the two olive trees
and the two lampstands
that stand before the Lord of the earth.
Revelation 11:3–4

Lord, what a powerful God You are!

December 28

"Let us rejoice and be glad and give the glory to Him,
for the marriage of the Lamb has come
and His bride has made herself ready."
Revelation 19:7

John the Baptist presented Jesus as the Lamb of God. Now John the Apostle reveals Christ again as the Lamb. This time He is preparing a supper in which His bride, "the Church," will be in the presence of the Lamb. This scene will take place in heaven, where the believers finally see Christ face-to-face.

December 29

And I saw another angel. . .having an eternal gospel
to preach to those who live on the earth. . .
and he said with a loud voice,
"Fear God, and give Him glory,
because the hour of His judgment has come;
worship Him who made the heaven
and the earth and sea and springs of waters."
Revelation 14:6–7

Lord, while there is still time, please provide imaginative ways in which we can speak forth Your Word of Truth to all those whom we love.

DECEMBER 30

And they sang the song of Moses the bond-servant
of God, and the song of the Lamb, saying,
"Great and marvelous are Your works,
O Lord God, the Almighty; Righteous
and true are Your ways,
King of the nations."
Revelation 15:3

Lord, You alone are worthy of our worship. I praise You with all my heart, and look forward to the day when I will worship You in heaven.

DECEMBER 31

There will no longer be any curse;
and the throne of God and of the Lamb will be in it,
and His bond-servants will serve Him;
they will see His face,
and His name will be on their foreheads.
Revelation 22:3–4

Lord, give me the courage to put the old year and its mistakes behind me. Let me grasp Your strong hand of forgiveness so that in Christ I might have not only a new year, but a brand-new life. Amen!

NOTES

Notes

NOTES

THE WAY TO JESUS CHRIST IS SIMPLE:

1. ADMIT THAT YOU ARE A SINNER.

For all have sinned, and come short
of the glory of God.
ROMANS 3:23

2. BELIEVE THAT JESUS IS GOD THE SON WHO PAID THE WAGES OF YOUR SIN.

For the wages of sin is death [eternal separation
from God]; but the gift of God is eternal life
through Jesus Christ our Lord.
ROMANS 6:23

3. CALL UPON GOD.

If thou shalt confess with thy mouth the Lord Jesus,
and shalt believe in thine heart that God hath raised him
from the dead, thou shalt be saved.
ROMANS 10:9

SALVATION IS A VERY PERSONAL THING
BETWEEN YOU AND GOD.
THE DECISION IS YOURS ALONE.